ISAAC BASHEVIS SINGER

Modern Literature Monographs

ISAAC BASHEVIS SINGER

Irving Malin

Frederick Ungar Publishing Co.
New York

Copyright © 1972 by Frederick Ungar Publishing Co., Inc.
Printed in the United States of America
Library of Congress Catalog Card Number: 73-185350
ISBN: 0-8044-2588-4 (cloth)

The discussion of *A Friend of Kafka* is partially taken from an article by the author that appeared in *Reconstructionist*, December 25, 1970, and is reprinted here by courtesy of that publication.

Contents

Chronology

I am indebted to the first chapter of Irving H. Buchen's *Isaac Bashevis Singer and the Eternal Past* (New York University Press, 1968) for many of the biographical details listed below. Mr. Singer has approved the accuracy of Buchen's chapter.

1904: Isaac Bashevis Singer was born on July 14, 1904 in Leoncin, Poland (the son of Bathsheba Zylberman, daughter of the Bilgoray rabbi, and Pinchos-Mendel Singer, a rabbi).

1907: He moved with his family to Radzymin, Poland after his father accepted the directorship of a *yeshivah* there.

1908: He moved to Warsaw, and observed his father as a judge of an ecclesiastical court. (These events are, of course, recorded in his memoirs.)

1914: He received *Crime and Punishment*, his first secular book, from his rationalist older brother, Israel Joshua.

1917: He became a *bar-mitzvah* (technically assuming manhood in Jewish religion). He traveled to Bilgoray with his mother and remained in the village until 1921. He decided there to write in Yiddish. He read Spinoza, Chekhov, Tolstoy, etc.

1921: He enrolled at the Tachkemoni Rabbinical Seminary in Warsaw, remaining there for a year.

1922: He returned to Bilgoray.

1923: He returned to Warsaw, remaining there for twelve

years. He became a proofreader for *Literarishe Bletter*, a Yiddish literary magazine.

1927:   He published his first work, a short story entitled "Women," in *Literarishe Bletter*. He also published two stories in *Warshawer Schriften*. He read Israel Joshua's first novel, *Blood Harvest*, published that same year.

1929:   His son, Israel, was born. (His first marriage, not a religious one, is not discussed at length by Singer.)

1933-1934:   He worked on the manuscript of *Satan in Goray*, his first novel which was accepted for serial publication by *Globus* and appeared in Yiddish in 1934.

1935:   *Satan in Goray* was published in book form by the Warsaw Yiddish P.E.N. Club. He moved to New York City and secured a free-lance position with the Yiddish newspaper *Forward*.

1940:   He married Alma, his present wife (after meeting her first in 1937).

1943:   *Satan in Goray and Other Tales* (including "The Destruction of Kreshev," "Zeidlus the Pope," etc.) was published in Yiddish by Farlag Maltones (New York).

1944:   He lost his brother and mentor, Israel Joshua, who died at the age of fifty-one.

1945-50:   He worked on *The Family Moskat* which appeared in serial form in the *Forward* from 1945-48 and was published in two volumes in Yiddish by Morris S. Sklarsky in 1950. The novel was translated into English and published by Alfred A. Knopf in 1950. It received the Louis Lamed Prize. He first became deeply involved with the English translations of his work.

1953:   His "Gimpel the Fool," translated into English by Saul Bellow, appeared in *Partisan Review*.

1954:   He met and became the friend of Cecil Hemley and his wife, Elaine Gottlieb (Hemley was editor of Noonday Press).

1955:   *Satan in Goray* was published by Noonday Press.
1957:   *Gimpel the Fool*, his first collection of stories, was published by Noonday. It was reviewed widely. Irving Howe wrote the first serious essay on his fiction.
1959:   He received a grant from the National Institute of Arts and Letters. He wrote and serialized *The Magician of Lublin* in the Yiddish *Forward*.
1960:   *The Magician of Lublin* was published by Noonday. In that year Noonday merged with Farrar, Straus and Giroux, his present publisher.
1961:   *The Spinoza of Market Street* was published. (Many of the stories had appeared in such wide circulation magazines as *Playboy* and *Saturday Evening Post* and such literary periodicals as *Chicago Review*.) He wrote and serialized *The Slave* in the *Forward*.
1962:   *The Slave* was published and became a best seller.
1963:   *Short Friday* was published.
1964:   He was elected to the National Institute of Arts and Letters, the only American member of the Institute to write in another language.
1966:   *In My Father's Court* was published. He was writer-in-residence at Oberlin.
1967:   *The Manor* was published. He was writer-in-residence at the University of California.
1968:   *The Séance* was published. He was writer-in-residence at the University of Wisconsin. The first book-length study of his work, *Isaac Bashevis Singer and the Eternal Past*, was written by Irving H. Buchen.
1969:   *The Estate* was published. Two collections of critical essays on Singer edited by Irving Malin and Marcia Allentuck were published. A pamphlet on Singer by Ben Siegel appeared.
1970:   *A Friend of Kafka* was published.

1

The

Memoirs

Isaac Bashevis Singer is an important American writer. Within the last twenty years he has broken through the language barrier—he continues to write in Yiddish, but he carefully supervises his English translations—so that he contributes regularly now to such magazines as *Playboy* and *The New Yorker*. His situation is wonderfully ironic. He is more well known than his older brother, Israel Joshua, author of *The Brothers Ashkanazi* (1936), who inspired him and was more popular before his death in 1944 than Isaac ever thought *he* could be.

I do not want here to document the biographical details of Singer's life. (I include a chronology at the beginning of this monograph.) However one point should be stressed. Although Singer arrived in America in 1935 (at the age of thirty-one), he remains haunted by the catastrophic events of his youth. His settings, for the most part, are in Polish cities or villages; his characters are familiar with orthodox Jewish rituals, books, holidays; his world is "exotic." But Singer is more than a provincial writer. He manages to transform his "special case" so that it becomes pertinent and universal. Surely the National Institute of Arts and Letters recognized this fact in 1964 when it elected him to membership; he is the only member to write in Yiddish or, indeed, in any foreign language.

Perhaps the best introduction to Singer is *In My Father's Court* (1966). In his author's note he informs us that these memoirs are the story "of a family and of a rabbinical court that were so close together that it was hard to tell where one ended and the other began."[1] The relationship of family and court—of private and universal worlds—is important because Singer demonstrates that one's life is "cosmic." Thus the memoirs move from "recollection" to historical event to univer-

sal law. The narrator is *a special case*—as is any autobio-
graphical narrator—but he is also a symbol of mysterious, all-embracing patterns. It is striking that Singer
spends much of his time in his preface on the philosophical and metaphysical assumptions of his father's
court, not on his own experiences (except in relation to
that court). He realizes—and makes us realize—that although we like to regard our lives as distinct and
unique, we are, after all, also playing roles in some
greater design. "Isaac Bashevis Singer" belongs to his
family, his religion, and his books.

"Why the Geese Shrieked" is a wonderful, representative chapter. It is a brief anecdote—the entire book
consists of such anecdotes—which begins with a statement about the nature of demons: "In our home there
was always talk about spirits of the dead that possess
the bodies of the living, souls reincarnated as animals,
houses inhabited by hobgoblins, cellars haunted by
demons."[2] This statement is significant for many reasons. Singer—or, better yet, the narrator—begins with
the general. The story which follows illustrates a message—about "our home" and the riddle of death. Already we understand that "I" cannot be separated from
"Other"; *no life stands alone.* The opening underlines
the narrator's persistent search—we refuse to call it
"obsessive," although it can be analyzed psychoanalyti-
cally—for the meaning of demons. We may be tempted
to see them merely as symbols of evil, but he insists
throughout the book that they are *real*, that they exist
as much as he does.

After the introduction, the narrator mentions his
father. The father speaks of demons because he reminds
his wife and children that "there are still mysterious
forces at work in the world."[3] He is the interpreter of
divine patterns, the holy storyteller. It is no wonder

that the narrator regards his memoirs—his own life—as a kind of religious parable. In this respect he carries on his father's tradition.

The father is not described at length. His physical condition is less important than his spiritual function. Immediately we recognize him as guide—"he told us a story that is found in one of the holy books."[4] His story is about demonic possession and painful exorcism of evil spirits. He becomes excited when one of his listeners questions the "truth" of this story. (The entire book will repeat this pattern as it questions the validity of complete acceptance of the father and his orthodox beliefs.)

The father does not have time to answer. In walks a woman carrying two geese. The abrupt entrance— we move from the story in the "holy books" to the "present" in Poland of the early 1900s—is thoroughly dramatic. But it is also functional; it suggests that times do not change radically, that people remain the same despite outward modifications of costume and custom. (Time is vague throughout these memoirs. We are never sure whether the narrator is six or eight or ten. We do not know the exact ages of his parents.) It is an "eternal" happening because it illustrates an ongoing story of faith.

The woman has an unusual problem; her geese make noises although they have been slaughtered! The stage is set for a conflict between the father and mother. Father trembles because he regards the geese as religious omens. But Mother, who comes from a family of rationalists, believes that there must be a nonmystical explanation. Of course, the narrator is torn. He does not know where to turn for advice; he is surrounded by stunned adults and shrieking geese.

The story ends abruptly. Mother pushes her slender finger inside the body of one goose and removes the windpipe, which had not really been removed. There is a rational reason for the shrieking! The narrator, however, prays "inwardly that the geese would shriek, shriek so loud that people in the street would hear and come running."⁵ His faith in his father's otherworldliness has been shaken.

I have explored this chapter in detail—it is only five pages long—because it introduces the basic tensions of the entire book: the conflict between orthodoxy and rationalism, the father and the mother. I emphasize the ambivalence felt by the narrator who is attracted to and repelled by the qualities incarnated in his parents. Singer is at his best here, refusing to settle for easy victory. (We remember the narrator's longing for the noise of the geese.) He moves gracefully from the "small" (or private) event to the large questions of faith.

The chapters rush past. In most of them the narrator continues to be ambivalent. He tells us, for example, in "A Gruesome Question" that he "was torn between two conflicting emotions. My fear dictated that I turn my eyes the other way, but my curiosity demanded just another glance. I knew that I would pay for each look with nightmares and torment, but each time anew, I leaned forward to see this living grave."⁶ (He is a visionary and he constantly stresses the "visual insight.") In "The Suicide" he hopes to learn from his father about Love and Death, but he is finally left alone with great mysteries. He plays cops and robbers outside, and becomes bored until he sees "a fiery flower, glittering like gold, luminous as the sun. It opened up like a chalice and bright colors leaped forth: yellow, green, blue, purple—colors and forms such as one sees only in a dream."⁷ He dangles between childhood and adulthood, the "court" and the outside world. He is suspended. I am not surprised that in "The Secret" he entertains the thought that he is not really the child of his father and mother.

The narrator searches everywhere for answers. In "To the Wild Cows" he goes on a trip to the countryside near Warsaw. He stares at a "real forest, full of wild animals and robbers"; he studies "butterflies of all colors."[8] He scrutinizes the sky, the sun, the clouds and "understands more clearly the meaning of the words of Genesis."[9] But this vision does not last. He gets lost; he stumbles upon a couple making love; he feels strangely abandoned. "To the Wild Cows" concludes with thoughts of home, "sadness and eeriness."[10]

The narrator turns to literature as another form of salvation. He heeds the advice of his older brother, Israel Joshua, and begins to read secular books. (He mentions his profound interest in *Crime and Punishment*.) He writes his own childish stories. When he visits Israel Joshua, who has fled from conscription into the army—the time is now that of World War I—he enters "the studio," a world entirely different from the court. (Even his rationalist mother would not be at home here.) He meets various artists, composers, and dancers. His fascination is readily apparent: they seem like "beings from a superior world."[11] Art is linked with nature—"through the skylight I could glimpse blue sky, sun and birds"[12]—and with sex. Although the studio is alien at first, it soon becomes a kind of "great good place"—to use Henry James' phrase. It is characteristic of the narrator to flee from complete acceptance of any one "house." "The Studio" ends not with images of health or wholeness but with tension. We are returned to the war—"nothing was as it should have been"[13]—and to the father's disgust with worldly literature.

The episodic structure of these memoirs continues. The narrator feels that he is the child of circumstances. *Things happen to him.* Although he is attracted to literature and nature—and, we must not forget, the religious orthodoxy of his father's court —he remains a shadowy creature. He is *ghostlike* (to use one of Singer's favorite adjectives) because he reflects the worlds he visits.

In the latter parts of the memoirs the narrator identifies with the ghostly victims of war. The German occupation creates hunger: prices increase and goods are depleted. Men roam everywhere. He writes that "the war demonstrated for me how unnecessary Rabbis were, my father among them. From all the towns and villages, Rabbis and other ecclesiastics converged on Warsaw, dejectedly walking the streets in their silk gabardines looking for a piece of bread."[14] (The scene is exceptionally vivid. Many of Singer's later fictions will deal with hunger. Food will become endowed with holiness.) Father's ghostlike behavior grows, but unlike his son, Father continues to study and to believe: "What else was there but the Torah?"[15]

The narrator finds nourishment as he begins to identify more strongly with his worldly brother. He studies the newspaper which employs Israel Joshua. (He even reads detective stories. Possibly he recognizes his quest for knowledge in Sherlock Holmes?) He admires him and his work. He gains more power through such identification. He becomes a young *man.* But he is, nevertheless, caught in the middle: "The chaos of the period and our desperate situation interrupted the fights between my father and brother, but they did not speak to each other."[16] He cannot give himself completely to either man.

"The Book" is an important chapter. Father decides to spend money to have his book "on the treatise of vows"[17] published. He asserts that it is more valuable than food. He informs his son about this secret. Although we are not really given the narrator's thoughts, we note one significant statement: "Now it seems to me that Father acted like any writer who wants to see his work in print."[18] I assume that by regarding his father as another writer, he can heal his wounds. *Father resembles Israel Joshua; he resembles both!* Such a union enables him to go ahead with his own writing (even though it pursues holiness in a "secular language," Yiddish). The psychological needs are under the surface here—as they are during the entire book—but they explain the miraculous ability of the narrator. They confirm his calling.

I do not want to impose any tight pattern upon these memoirs, but I think that it is meaningful for the narrator to devote his last fifty pages to his spatial (and psychological?) separation from his father and Israel Joshua. After "The Book" we read "The Visa." The narrator goes on a trip to Bilgoray: "Our situation was such that we could no longer remain in Warsaw. Since the summer of 1915, we had been constantly hungry. Father was again writing and had become the head of a yeshivah . . . but his salary wasn't large enough even to buy bread."[19] Bilgoray is the birthplace of his mother. Here he will be reborn away from the tensions of the men in his life. He does not feel guilty—as his mother does—about his departure, especially after he is urged to leave: "I was too young and giddy to understand Mother's self-recriminations and doubts."[20]

"The Journey" begins. The narrator is delighted once more by the beautiful countryside: the wheat, the apple orchards, the potatoes. He feels free of the Warsaw tensions—his last view of Israel Joshua is that of a "smaller" figure on the train platform—and learns to appreciate the down-to-earth knowledge of Mother. *She becomes his interpreter, as it were, and she possesses soothing answers.* Bilgoray, like her, is bountiful: "The fields were all shapes and colors, squares and rectangles, dark green and yellow. . . . I wished I could stay there forever."[21]

Bilgoray, he soon discovers, is not really paradise. The narrator finds that the "old Jewishness"—a chapter title—is more evident here than in Warsaw, but it cannot completely prevent victories of the "evil spirit": two Jewish sisters become whores; the heretical, secular views of sons displease their fathers; proponents of enlightenment attract him. The narrator reduced "everything to dust, proclaiming that life was worthless and the noblest thing a man could do was kill himself. I was fifteen, pale. . . ."[22] (The year is 1919.)

The memoirs end with a chapter entitled "The New Winds." We learn in the first sentence that "upheaval marked Bilgoray, for so long successfully obscured from the world by my grandfather."[23] The winds of Zionism, secularism, and enlightenment shake the town and narrator. His calling as a writer torn between two worlds is reaffirmed as he reads Spinoza, who becomes for him a symbol of the nonorthodox Jew who, nevertheless, carries his heritage.

He is exalted by the philosophical insistence upon pantheism: "It seemed to me that the truths I had been seeking since childhood had at last become apparent. . . . Everything was divine, everything was thought and extension."[24] The narrator fuses (or thinks he comprehends the fusing of) Heaven and Earth. He desires to learn and write. He becomes a Hebrew teacher for the children in the village.

He has come full circle. Now the narrator emerges as a reflection of his father, the Rabbi, but he will not believe fully in his traditions. *He holds "court" in the outside world.* Thus he also reflects the secularism of Israel Joshua—he will teach by writing worldly books. And Mother? Doesn't he find nourishment in her family and village and, most of all, in her skeptical wisdom?

In My Father's Court is an even more complex book than I have indicated. It is an introduction to the persistent themes and symbols of Singer's fiction, but it stands alone as the glowing account of a writer's birth. It suggests that literature arises from creative unrest and ambivalence; that it flourishes best when it reflects the childhood needs of the writer, and that it is, finally, a kind of salvation in the absence of orthodox religion.

2

The

Open

Novels

Singer's fiction can be divided into three categories: the open novels, the closed novels, and the short stories. Although he deals with the recurring themes which are stated in a personal "shorthand" in his memoirs—he is, after all, an obsessive writer—he structures them in different ways. This is not to assert that he is a radical innovator in the manner of a Joyce or Proust. He tends to use traditional structures because they can mirror the religious themes of tradition and anti-tradition.

Singer has written three open novels: *The Family Moskat* (1950), *The Manor* (1967), and *The Estate* (1969). I use the adjective "open" to denote that these long works are broadly conceived; that they describe many families and events in a comprehensive way to cover the unlimited range of human experience. Their openness is one of *scope*—vast distances, wide differences of age (and time), and panoramic space; it forces us to be aware of sweeping strokes, not minute details.

The Family Moskat deals with the years from about 1910 to 1939 and with three generations of Polish Jews. Old values and rituals—incarnated in Hasidic (Chasidic) joy—give way to secular movements of Zionism, socialism, or Enlightenment. The conflicts between traditional and modern Jew are viewed largely as generational disputes—sons (and grandsons) fight their fathers. (There is, of course, the added conflicts between Jews and Gentiles.) The main effect of all the battles is summarized by Ben Siegel's remarks: "With mounting uncertainty and disillusionment, Orthodox Hasidim bitterly debate Zionists, socialists, cosmopolites, and an increasingly aggressive middle class. Oblivious to the forthcoming catastrophe [the beginning of World War II], all dissipate their energies in internecine quarrels succeeding only in losing

God without winning the world."[1]

The Family Moskat begins with a leisurely description of the return of Reb Meshulam Moskat and his third wife, Rosa (and her daughter Adele) to Warsaw. Reb Meshulam is an old, wealthy Jew who controls the destinies of his many children, grandchildren, and the Jewish community itself. Ironically his power isolates him from the others. "Many unusual stories had been told about him"[2] in the past and now the general feeling is that he is an old goat. His new marriage symbolizes his decline and also introduces the many sexual tensions throughout the novel. Thus Singer begins with marriage, unity, "togetherness"—the words apply not only to the private life of the Moskats but to the Jews in Warsaw—and then gradually alerts us to separation and fragmentation. (The pattern resembles that of *In My Father's Court*. It is possible, indeed, to see Reb Meshulam as a worldly reflection of the narrator's father in the memoirs—both men lose their authority with the passage of time.)

Chapter Two introduces us to another traveler, a stranger of nineteen named Asa Heshel Bannet. (The entire novel is, as we would expect, full of symbolic entrances and exits.) The contrasts are clear. Asa is unworldly, innocent, and philosophical; his limitations (or strengths?) are deliberately counterposed to those of Reb Meshulam Moskat. But Singer does not stop with such contrasts; he compels us to note that despite their outward differences, both men are seeking some revelation which will enable them to live fully. They are secretly searching for the Messiah.

I stress their spiritual quest. Singer makes it clear that they (especially Asa) cannot be satisfied with materialistic delights; they must come to terms with their Jewishness. They must define it—if only to survive in an increasingly alien, fragmented world. When Asa eventually meets the Moskats, he listens to a conversation between Hadassah, Reb Meshulam's granddaughter (whom he eventually marries), and other members of the clan. It circles about the idea of assimilation. Here are some pertinent passages of dialogue: "Back in Austria, Jews and gentiles live together like one family. . . ." "Well, to tell the truth, when you take a look at all these Warsaw Jews, in their long gabardines and skullcaps, it's as though you found yourself in China all of a sudden."[3] These sentences illuminate the breakdown of communication *within the same family and the same religion.* Asa discovers that he is on his own; he must define and create his Jewishness before he can be saved or save himself. (He is like the narrator of *In My Father's Court,* who also seeks a new faith in the midst of tense ambivalence and incompletion.)

Singer constantly relates the Moskats (and later the Bannets) to their religious heritage. *They are always celebrating.* Chapter Four of Part One begins: "Meshulam Moskat had long made it a practice to distribute the seasonal gifts to his family directly after the ritual of blessing the first Chanukah candle."[4] The family get-together becomes linked in our minds with joyous festivals; the association is underlined because when all of the Moskats begin to fight openly, we sense the "universal" implications: the cosmic design begins to crack.

Again there are structural contrasts. Chapter Five, unlike the previous one describing the Moskats at home, presents a lengthy description of the Hasidim at Bialodrevna, a village close to Warsaw.[5] (We remember Bilgoray as a temporary refuge in the memoirs.) At first these orthodox believers seem to be com-

pletely unlike the Moskats; however, they also feel
the new winds (although they cannot acknowledge
these). "The rabbi's tall figure was bent."[6] His symbolic position indicates that he is shaken by his daughter's departure for Warsaw. He thinks: "Here in Poland, Satan roamed openly through the streets. Youths
were running away from the study houses, shaving off
their beards, eating the unclean food of the gentile."[7]
He blames himself and his followers, not the heavenly
Father. It is ironic that he is soon asked for some spiritual advice by Reb Meshulam.

Thus the novel traces the steady decline of orthodox belief. Reb Meshulam grows sick, lies on his death
bed, and regrets the way he has spent his life. He realizes that his family and community will not uphold
his values; he regrets everything now. He broods over
a passage from Ecclesiastes: "All is vanity and vexation
of spirit." Asa, unable to follow the Hasidic values
of his own grandfather, turns to worldly books—to the
sciences in particular—and to "Love" (first with Hadassah and later Adele) as a new faith. But such rela-
tionships bring pain and unfulfillment. (Throughout
the novel marriage fails to provide salvation.) And the
minor characters, who are frequently introduced to
stress the problems of Asa, find that other "modern"
solutions and faiths are not worthwhile. Abram, a son-
in-law of Reb Meshulam, puts the matter concisely:
"Everything we Jews do we do lopsided. We match a
flea with an elephant. And what come out are cripples,
schlemiels, lunatics. Ah, the Exile, the Exile! It's de-
moralized us."[8]

Reb Meshulam's funeral becomes an important
symbolic event. We recognize the death of the old
order and the birth of modern confusion. Every Jew
is a spectator and participant: "The spectators from

the balconies and windows were afraid that the crowd passing forward in the cemetery would overturn the hearse, or that some of the rabble would be pushed into the open grave."⁹ Rabbis mourn at length; the modern Moskat granddaughters worry about their clothing; and the sons go their special ways.

It is appropriate that after the funeral Asa Heshel becomes the "hero." I put quotes around the word "hero" for several reasons. Is he really superior to the other characters in the novel? Does he stand alone as an example? Is he hero or anti-hero? Does Singer, indeed, believe in heroism? I am unsure about the answers to all of these questions. Although Asa is an archetypal Jewish intellectual adrift in the world, he is not completely characterized. He is almost a stereotype: rebel against tradition, seeker after truth, good-bad husband and lover. He remains obscure despite the growing attention he merits. Perhaps this is Singer's shrewd design. Asa's questionable heroism reminds us *that the Jew in exile cannot function heroically. His identity flourishes only in relation to his people and his Lord. When he forsakes these, he is incomplete, obsessive and half-alive.* I do not mean to imply that Singer presents an orthodox view. He is modern enough—remember his memoirs!—to realize that new patterns must be shaped, but he also understands that these have to confront old ones.

The novel raises these questions in a rather "old-fashioned" manner. Asa is *manipulated* to engage in lengthy conversations about Jewish destiny. These almost dominate the scene. It is probably fair to say that Singer believes in a union of conversation (idea) and action, that Asa cannot act properly unless he learns by dialogue his true nature. Although I appreciate the reason for the extended philosophical conversations, I am not moved by them because they seem programmed and artificial. They are, curiously, less alive than such action-filled scenes as Reb Meshulam's funeral. Here, for example, is part of a conversation between Asa and his rabbinic grandfather: "Asa Heshel made an answer to the effect that Jews were a people like every other people, and that they were demanding that the nations of the world return the Holy Land to them. But the rabbi was far from satisfied. If, he insisted, they had no further belief in the Bible, then why should they have any longing for the Biblical land of the Jews? Why not some other country?"[10] Obviously the conversation (reported as Asa hears it) is significant, but it is almost gratuitous because it merely repeats, without much clarification, positions and actions already taken. It is *false underlining*, as it were, and it impedes the flow of events.

Singer is at his best when he allows the sudden vision to occur. Asa and the other Jews are best defined as they unexpectedly glimpse the nature of their condition. Their revelations are *inexplicable;* they are beyond preaching. Reb Dan, who had engaged his grandson Asa in the lengthy conversation quoted above, discovers after World War I begins that his own faith is in peril. He shouts angrily: "Enough! It is time! High time for the Messiah!"[11] (Is it a misreading of his character to suggest that he cannot be completely secure in his prayers?) Asa sits in his army camp —he is one of the few Jews—and carries "on a dispute with Spinoza."[12] He tries to accept the *necessity* of everything that is happening. His painful struggle ends inconclusively. The Germans enter Warsaw. Reb Meshulam's son-in-law Abram tries to say something to one of the invading guards at the train station and is flung to the gutter: " 'Get the hell out of here, you

damn Jew!' The soldier made a threatening gesture
with his gun."[13] These three revelatory passages—the
gun, the copy of Spinoza, the hope for the Messiah—
share one quality: they affirm that real truths are
earned *painfully and instantly*.

I take this fact to be one of the most interesting
things in the novel. Although many critics have cited
the flow of time—it does not require much critical so-
phistication to notice this quality—they have neglected
to mention that in this time-filled work, there are overwhelming "moments" in which time stops and eternal
truths emerge. Singer gives us "still points," recognizing that only when Asa removes himself from the growing confusion and decline of the Moskats and Bannets,
does he gain knowledge. I do not want to overstate
these still points. Singer is not, after all, a Christian
mystic. He realizes that we are trapped by history—
by family and heritage—and that the most we can do
is to understand the nature of our destiny. But he suggests that we have the free will to learn. His still points
are profoundly educational, ahistorical and historical
at the same time.

The war continues; the Moskats surrender to assimilation, secularism, and occasionally heresy. Family
chaos; political chaos; private chaos—who can find
cause and effect? Singer will not take the convenient
way; he refuses to accept one cause as the prime
mover. It is true that he condemns the self-love of
Asa and Reb Meshulam, but he does not regard it as
completely demonic. Perhaps he is like Job. He realizes that the mysteries remain despite all of the schemes
we create for understanding, and that we are finally
in the dark. (This does not mean that we should court
foolishness or remain aloof.) He does not resemble
Asa, his "hero," because he sees beyond his groping—

his knowledge of the "unknowable" has come after much thought—and he gives us several passages, if not the entire novel, to demonstrate Asa's limitations. Abram and Asa converse at one point about "life, liberty, and the pursuit of happiness." The hero has observed much bloodshed; he is "blinded." He says about the Lord: "You can't see His wisdom when you look at a tortured child, all covered with lice, or when you're squeezed into a cattle car and you have to do your needs through a window."[14] We have suffered along with him, and we are tempted to accept his finality of vision (or vision of finality?). Singer cannot do so. He makes Abram ask: "Suppose some good comes from all this evil?"[15] The conversation does not end here, but it should. Only a question can answer Asa's finality.

I find that the unanswered question is a key to Singer's technique in this novel. He refuses to settle for comforting answers—the Jews deserve to die (Asa's view at one point); there is no plan to the universe— and he will not assign victory to chance, destiny, or free will. Singer believes all three are mysteriously joined, but he even questions this vision. He shuns "final solutions." He is beyond answers.

Time passes; the characters age (but, strangely enough, remain the same); life comes and goes. It is now the 1930s. The Bialodrevna Hasidim have been forced to move to Warsaw—we remember how they appeared once to be removed from urban ills!—but they continue to believe in their orthodox faith. They prepare the Passover matzos "in the strict ritual manner."[16] At the *seder* the Moskats gather and proclaim the traditional words: "Slaves were we unto Pharaoh in Egypt." Although some of them accept their Jewishness, others cannot repeat the words without wondering whether they are enough. Asa looks on and broods: "They were all doomed."[17] Hitler is, for him, more than another Pharaoh or Haman; he will put an end to such "meaningless" religious festivals.

Singer compels us to ask many questions. Can religious values exist after the gathering holocaust? Is there any relation between festivals (even such signifi- cant ones as Passover) and the day-to-day life of "doomed" Jews? Do the Nazis represent a break with history? Are the Jews entering a new age in which their religion cannot function? How should Jewish- ness be defined? Such large questions, which have lurked in the background, demand to be answered. Only Asa is willing to confront them. After the *seder*, he hopes for consolation from his beloved Spinoza. But even Spinoza cannot help—how can Hitler be re- garded as part of the cosmic design? "If one was logi- cally consistent, then one had to concede that God was evil, or else that suffering and death were good."[18] Asa must move beyond logic (as I have suggested that Singer does).

He takes the first steps. During the flight with Barbara (his Marxist girlfriend), he suddenly chants a line from the Psalms: "I will lift up mine eyes unto the hills, from whence cometh my help." But the help does not come. He continues to rage about his people and their burdens (not realizing that he is, in fact, acting in the way his ancestors did). At least he rec- ognizes his illogical nature.

The bombs burst around Asa, destroying every- thing that once sustained him and the Moskats. (Or so he feels.) Where can he turn now? Who can help ex- plain things? How can he survive—not as a "hero" but as a *living person?*

Asa has changed. He is still asking questions as he

did at nineteen, but he knows that they cannot really be answered *on earth at this time*. No Messiah will appear to supply the truth. In the last lines of the novel he asks typically: "What do you mean?"[19] But his heart is not in the question. He receives the answer—the English translation, but not the Yiddish original, of the novel concludes here—that "Death is the Messiah. That's the real truth."[20] We do not see his response, but we know enough about him (and Singer) to affirm that he is beyond such easy truth.

And this movement is surely established by the structure of the novel. *The Family Moskat* shapes art to conform to life—people appear and disappear; coincidences abound; time jumps and moves slowly; the *flow* continues. Thus it proclaims that no one worldly philosophy can suffice to explain the ebb and flow of human life. It does more. It suggests, ironically enough, that art—even high art such as this very novel!—cannot fully capture existence on earth. *It profoundly questions itself.*

The ironies do not stop here. Singer implies that the Jew is somehow defined by his ability *to remain open to questions*—that he is *the open man*, as it were. *The Family Moskat* is, by its very form, a plea for openness and, consequently, Jewishness. It is able to describe the "death" of Warsaw (the old and new order) and yet, miraculously, to go beyond death to hope. It thereby criticizes and affirms Jewish religion.

The Manor and *The Estate* take us back to nineteenth-century Poland. Social and religious values are in great disorder. The Polish noblemen, who tried unsuccessfully to rebel against Russian domination, lose their power (and manors); the Jews discover, at least for the time being, a degree of prosperity as they assume control of manors. But such material success compels many Jews to divorce themselves from their religious traditions.

Calman Jacoby is the center of *The Manor*. He gains wealth but watches his daughters go in different directions. Shaindel marries Ezriel Babad, son of a rabbi, who is an assimilationist like Asa Heschel Bannet. Miriam converts to Catholicism when she marries Count Jampolski's crazy son. (His other two daughters marry orthodox Jews.) Calman tries to keep his traditional beliefs after his sudden "rise" (and necessary business entanglements with non-Jews) and the death of his wife, but as we shall see, he succeeds only with great difficulty, especially after his unhappy marriage to "modern" Clara Kaminer.

Ezriel becomes the inverse reflection of Calman. He moves to the center of the stage (in the second novel) after he begins to understand the folly of his assimilation and science. His love affair, after his wife Shaindel goes mad (an ironic detail because he is a psychiatrist!), is presented as one example of the limitation of modern substitutes for religion.

Both novels reflect the breakdown of marriage (and community life), but the end of *The Estate* offers a sense of freedom and order as Ezriel and Calman, in their strikingly different ways, *accept their fate as Jews*. Calman is orthodox; Ezriel is "reformed" (in his view of Jewishness as history rather than theology) —the significant idea is that they are finally *believers in, not rebels against, tradition*. (The novels themselves are old-fashioned chronicles.) The manor (or material success) falls; acceptance of human limitations reigns.

The Manor "portrays an earlier period—the epoch between the Polish insurrection of 1863 and the end of the nineteenth century . . .";[21] but it continues to employ the same themes and structures as *The Family Moskat.*

Chapter One begins swiftly with the unsuccessful 1863 rebellion against the Czar by Polish noblemen: peasants remove their caps and women weep as Count Jampolski is led through town to prison. It is, obviously, another time of *change*—as it was at the beginning of *The Family Moskat.* In the absence of the Count, Calman Jacoby, a "Jew of some standing who dealt in wheat and traded with the manor, obtained from the village officials the name of the new lord of the Jampolski manor."[22] The way down is the way up (or vice versa); history is a seesaw; apparently people are driven, unless they are able to exert spiritual discipline.

The first chapter indicates Calman's sense of order. He is a religious, polite, and decorous man; he believes that there are proper laws. Although he advances swiftly, he does not at first lose control of the situation; he refuses to have his household corrupted by current fashions. He continues to pray at dawn.

Singer's style moves briskly, alerting us to details (which are religious signs), but it also *measures* the changing times. It mirrors authoritative Calman, refusing to yield to bravura or obsessive designs. Here is one paragraph which, although shorter than most, perfectly characterizes the union of style and "heroic" temperament: "Calman Jacoby prospered rapidly. Though not yet forty, he was already wealthy. No great scholar, he could just about manage to find his way through some of the simpler parts of the Talmud. Nevertheless, he was esteemed for his piety, honesty, and shrewdness."[23] We can see that Singer is less interested in physical details than in moral (religious) qual-

ities. Calman may wear a certain kind of coat; he may
have long sidelocks—these details which are mentioned, by the way, in the next paragraph are only significant as they symbolize his beliefs. *Calman prospers,
but his prosperity is not dwelt upon, except as it relates to his piety*. The representative paragraph moves
swiftly from material to spiritual assets.

There is one other revealing characteristic here.
Singer uses the word "rapidly." He does not define it.
He does not tell us *exactly* how fast Calman prospers
(or indeed how old he is). He regards time as less important than eternity. (We have noted this fact in the
books already discussed.) Thus he writes a historical
novel which implies that time itself for Jews cannot be
divorced from religion. He is giving us religious history (a paradoxical phrase); it assumes that although
times and men change, they remain fundamentally the
same. By the end of the first chapter (or, better yet,
by the end of the first section of that chapter), we
know much about Calman's psychology and religion.
The suspense in the rest of the novel lies in the relationship of his prosperity to his piety. Will he change?
Should Jews live in the manor (the symbol of worldly
wealth)? Can religion remain steadfast? Should it
"progress"?

Singer introduces other characters who act as foils
to Calman. Perhaps the most important one is Ezriel,
his future son-in-law. When we first meet him, he is
reciting a Talmudic text and interpreting it. Although
he wears "full Hassidic dress," he does not "look like a
typical Hassid."[24] The details, as usual, are carefully
chosen for their symbolic qualities. Ezriel is both in
and out of the orthodox tradition accepted by Calman.
He rebels against the "typical"; he *interprets* for him-

self. He clearly resembles Asa Bannet and Israel Joshua, especially when Singer gives us some of the "enlightened" questions the young man asks: "Was Adam a Jew?"[25] Ezriel is interrupted during his studies—he has been immersed in a chapter on forbidden impurities!—by the announcement that Calman Jacoby is ready to offer his daughter's hand in marriage.

Marriage functions again as a symbol of conflict, disunity, and fragmentation. When Ezriel makes clear his rationalistic views during the courtship of Shaindel, she and Calman are shocked, but they believe that marriage will change him. But it does not. He continues to rebel; he acts as though he were single.

Family ties are constricting to him (and to the other characters). Whenever we have a celebration described at length, for example, we note great conflict. The "hostile feasts" resemble those of *The Family Moskat*. Ezriel quarrels with Calman, claiming that although "Jews always remember God . . . , God forgets the Jews."[26] Miriam Lieba, one of Calman's daughters, thinks at some other time that "She'd bear children, wrangle with her mother-in-law, grow old before her time."[27] She, like Ezriel, is attracted to the outside world. At the end of Part One of the novel, she runs away—to the Gentile—and her flight is the culmination of the various rebellions against marriage, the family, and the old order. But Calman has the last word for the time being; his legs almost buckle under him, but he recites a passage from scripture: "The Lord hath given and the Lord hath taken away."

Part Two begins with a quick notation: "Two years passed."[28] Within that span of time, the various characters have acted in representative ways. Ezriel moved to Warsaw, the big city, to study; Calman worked hard and prayed earnestly; Shaindel gave birth. Now time speeds up and the underlying tensions accelerate rapidly.

Calman repeats the folly of Reb Meshulam Moskat. He finds that he cannot remain alone after his wife's death: "Sooner or later he would have to remarry."[29] He longs for a son to perpetuate his name. He begins to lose his total commitment; his self-love— yes, even he has some of this quality!—tortures him. He falls in love with the sophisticated, neurotic Clara Kaminer. But is it love? Or is he merely infatuated with the idea that he can *afford* her? Singer does not inform us. Their marriage is doomed—like most of the others in the novel. Calman realizes this fact as he tries to flee from the ceremony: " 'Is there any way out? What must I do, according to the law?' Calman knew the answer: he must stand up and run as if a fire were chasing him. He must fast, repent, and torture himself for the sins he had committed."[30] Although he has yielded to temptations of love (or self-love?), he remains curiously righteous. His faith reasserts itself even more strongly than before.

Perhaps this is the fictional problem with Calman. He apparently *changes*—he prospers; he yields to Clara; he tries to see that his daughters are married—*but he remains such a "simple," pious person that he cannot sustain the burden of the novel.* He lacks "heroism"— unless we redefine it as the ability to accept the old order. He does not radically question things.

Ezriel is, as I have suggested, an inverse reflection. He constantly questions; he moves out of "accepted" boundaries; he strays. But even his more modern qualities tend to be somewhat simple. We know that whenever we meet him, he will demonstrate *the same qualities. He will not surprise us.* We are right. In Part Two,

for example, we see him again at study: he reads and
ponders the nature of good and evil. His outward appearance and occupation may have changed, but these
are after all less important than his inherent questioning
attributes.

Temptation arises in Ezriel's case as it does in Calman's. (Most of Singer's fictions center upon the
temptations of sex and worldliness.) He decides to
study medicine and to make his way in the Gentile
world. The conversation between him and Wallenberg,
a convert to Catholicism, is especially revealing. Wallenberg urges him to forget Polish Jews, a "tribe of
Asiastics,"[31] and to enter polite society. Perfect man-
ners are important when one has social aspirations. Ezriel realizes that although he may dislike his heritage,
he cannot really surrender it. Like Asa Bannet he is
ambivalent. He rages against Jewishness because it is
not as perfect as it *could or should be*.

While Ezriel worries about his possible conversion, Calman tries to regain fully his simple piety. His
marriage to Clara is dreadful—in the old sense—because
she is a free spirit who "dismissed his help and hired
her own, wrangled with the neighboring landowners. . . ."[32] She is a more dangerous Wallenberg, trying to tempt him with the sexual pleasures of
"Gentile" life. The most touching scenes of the novel
show us Calman isolated at home; his wife and son oc-
cupy a different world. Sasha, his son, is a "savage"; he
calls his father "a dirty Jew." The ironies are profound here. Calman is, indeed, "a dirty Jew" because
he has temporarily yielded to lust and given up his
sense of wholeness. He hits Sasha, really wanting to
destroy himself.

Part Two ends with the growing separation and
violence in the lives of Calman and Ezriel. Unable to

find meaning in marriage or occupations, they continue to search for truth as they conceive it. In the last line Calman thinks: "It was not death that he wanted, however, but the life of a Jew."[33] The phrase bears repeating—the "life of a Jew." How does one live as a Jew? Does he become a Jew only after yielding to the temptations of the outside world? Can he be a Jew without his Lord?

The novel has been structured dialectically. We would expect Part Three to resolve these questions, to supply the synthesis, and to give us wholeness once more.

It begins, interestingly, with Clara. Although I have not discussed her at length, I should suggest that she is more (or less) than an evil temptress. At times she seems to possess a stronger will than any of the men in the novel; at other times she freezes into immobile passivity. She is a truly warped creature. Singer does not know what to do with her. He condemns her quest for sexual freedom, but he also admires her independence and shrewdness. I think the suspense generated at the end of Part Two is dissipated. Clara is so fascinating that she interferes with the spiritual dilemmas of the hero. Or is Singer fooling us? Perhaps he wants us to *surrender* to her (as Calman did) so that we can recognize her attractions and then reject them.

Clara is one way out of Jewishness. Contrasted to her in Part Three (and really throughout the novel) is the Hassidic community of Marshinov. (It is like Bilgoray in the memoirs.) Jochanan, a son-in-law of Calman's, is diametrically opposed to her and to the enlightened Ezriel. He deems himself constantly unworthy; he retreats from the world, staying in his study and tormenting himself with such questions as: "Shouldn't he go into exile and fast and castigate himself—in summer prick himself with thorns, in winter roll in the snow?"[34] Jochanan is, perhaps, as extreme as Clara and what she represents. In his continual despair and his flight from the "manor," he can offer little salvation for the tortured, "moderate" Calman.

Calman is alone for most of Part Three. He walks in the Marshinov snow; he does not want to return to the manor. "What awaited him at home? An adulteress and an ungovernable child. He was no longer young. He had had his fill of business."[35] Quite a change! Previously he had defined himself as a Jew, father, and businessman. Now he has only his religion to guide him. Unlike Jochanan, he does not use it to help him escape from reality. He is not fanatical (or obsessive). He prays for a meaningful revelation—one which will help him to live more fully.

Singer deliberately interrupts Calman's quest—as he does throughout the novel—to describe the noisy, catastrophic, public world: "Events moved swiftly. Catastrophes, coming one on top of the other, recalled the passage from the Book of Job about the messengers with evil tidings. It started with the bomb thrown at Alexander II, followed by the pogroms in Warsaw."[36] We are not surprised to meet Ezriel in this chapter. He belongs to this world, although he fights against its violence. He is now a specialist in nervous diseases; he has "converted" to psychiatry, as many Jews did, but he realizes that he can never completely surrender his heritage, his angle of vision. We see Ezriel alone (like Calman), pacing in his office and wondering about modern chaos: "Existence had always meant the same chaos; the ego had always wanted everything for itself—money, fame, sex, knowledge, power, immortality. But this savage was constantly coming up against the resistance of the world with its restrictions and taboos. Was it any wonder that people went mad?"[37]

It is ironic that Ezriel falls in love (with the briefly-introduced Olga Bielikov) after his lengthy comments about the savage ego. He may know the "right" answers, but he lacks the will to follow them. He wavers; he cannot sustain himself. He is, metaphorically, doctor *and* patient at the same time.

"Love" is not the final answer. Immediately after Ezriel's first affair we read more about Clara (now divorced from Calman) and her lover, Zipkin. Their arguments, desertions, and tensions are not made to appear especially attractive. They are "mad" (like Ezriel and, in another way, Jochanan). They are so involved with their ego-designs that they cannot function adequately in the public or religious world. They are drowning.

I think that Singer wants to stress such madness before he returns finally to Calman in the last chapter. Although our hero is not deep or complex enough to bear the weight of the novel, as I have mentioned previously, his steadiness is particularly imposing now. His rhythms are peaceful; he is in tune with some higher serious music. Note the beginning paragraph: "Calman Jacoby was sixty-five. There had been a time when he had thought he would be dead by that age. According to the Talmud, a man who reaches the age when his parents died should begin to think about his own demise."[38] The slow pace; the reflective simplicity —such qualities help us to understand and appreciate *humility*. And this is precisely Singer's great achievement. Calman may not be as "alive" as exciting (or excited) Ezriel, but he exemplifies humility to such a great extent, especially after he escapes from excitement, that he becomes a memorable *witness*.

There is one other virtue he possesses. Perhaps it is the cause of humility? Calman realizes that he is part of the tradition; he is not really unique. His ego is less important than his super-ego. He regards himself as a reflection of "generations of ancestors." *He is another Jew.* It is finally his "marriage" with the spiritual leaders and scholars which, unlike his marriage to Clara, gives him a sense of wholeness (and holiness): "They argued with him as to what was right and what was wrong, what was pure and impure. They made him a kind of partner in sharing the Torah's treasures. Among these shelves of sacred books, Calman felt protected. Over each volume hovered the soul of its author. In this place, God watched over him."[39]

The Estate is the sequel to *The Manor* and, like the earlier novel, it employs a three-part structure.

Part One begins with the sudden illness of Daniel Kaminer, Clara's father. I am less interested in his characterization—he played a relatively minor role in *The Manor*—than in the symbolic introduction. The novel begins with illness and death (unlike the earlier book, which described Calman's "rise"), and it insists upon mortality, man's "estate": "But when you were dying, nothing mattered."[40] Kaminer leaves his business to Sasha, his grandson.

We again meet Clara and Ezriel. Their various love affairs are unsettling. Ezriel spends an idyllic period with Olga Bielikov in the country; by doing so, he helps to drive Shaindel, his wife, out of her mind. The tensions between men and women parallel, if on a more superficial level, the tensions between men and their religion. It is interesting to note that Ezriel and Clara (and, as we have seen, Calman in his brief fall) cannot find happiness in love or orthodox belief. *They cannot commit themselves; they lack the strength to surrender their ego-designs.* They are curiously helpless.

Singer uses "madness" as a recurring symbol in the novel. Ezriel treats mad patients and he is married to one. Shaindel "developed a persecution mania and complained that Ezriel wanted to kill her . . . Although Shaindel knew nothing about Olga, she spoke of another woman, whom Ezriel would marry after Shaindel's death."[41] Later he thinks: "What a misfortune to deal all day with the madness of strangers and at night come home to an insane wife!"[42] The ironies are more complex. Ezriel himself is "mad"—he surrenders to whims, delusions, designs—and his condition, "normal" though it may be, contributes, no doubt, to Shaindel's illness. There is, as he himself admits, a logic in her madness. There is an added turn of the screw. Ezriel wants to view madness as "the law of life"[43]—his phrase. In an earlier discussion with his son, he reveals that anti-semitism and nationalism are examples of madness. He reduces complicated movements and ideas to "simple" illness. Such reduction is his own disease. By considering the world as an asylum—and there is no doubt that often it seems to be one!—he can indulge himself. He says to his son: "How can one fight madness? There's no cure. That is the truth."[44]

Singer, obviously, does not agree with him. He believes, instead, that "madness" is frequently an excuse for passivity, selfishness, and evil in general. After describing Ezriel, he turns to the sermon delivered by Calman's son-in-law, Jochanan, at the village of Marshinov. There is one enlightening passage: "War expresses anger; love, kindness. What connection is there between the two? And how can one wage love? The answer is that man is born to serve. If he does not

serve God, he serves man."[45] Madness results (in Jochanan's view) from slavery to man (including one-
self), not from slavery to the Lord. It is, consequently,
a symptom of *evil*. Calman appreciates his son-in-law's
sermon. He has moved beyond slavery to man (beyond
madness) to firm faith: "He had committed enough
transgressions, had raised bad children. Some of his
grandchildren were Gentiles. Woe unto him, he had
left no Jewish male descendant for Sasha was a
heathen."[46]

There is one conversation between Calman and
Clara which revolves about the theme of madness and
faith. She wants him to take care of her illegitimate
child by Zipkin. He refuses. Their words are at cross-
purposes. They exist in different worlds of discourse.
"Madness" obviously means different things for them.
The following passage sums up their conflicting worlds;
it stresses their mutual strangeness: "Calman shivered.
His eyes bulged as he looked at her. There was something different about her, a blend of insolence and
coarseness in her expression that hadn't been there when
she had been his wife. She stared back at him with the
viciousness and curiosity with which beasts sometimes
examine a human being."[47]

Part Two concentrates upon the affairs of Clara
and Ezriel. It does not advance our understanding; it
tries to show that they become even more desperate
and confused as they live longer. Probably the most
sustained pieces of writing occur when Singer dwells
upon passing (or passed) time. We get vivid intima-
tions of mortality.

Clara visits New York and meets her old lover.
They barely recognize each other. They have been
assaulted by time—they have seen their mortal estate:
"Clara stood up, her feet numb. She looked at him. It

was Zipkin, but older, his hair no longer thick. At the top of his closely cropped head there was a bald spot sprouting fuzz like swamp grass. His brows had grown together and he squinted myopically. Two wrinkles bordered his mouth, indicating the impatient bitterness of one who does things against his will. He had not recognized her!"[48] Consider the next-to-last sentence. Zipkin is not the only one who dislikes submitting to others and to life itself—Clara and Ezriel also rebel against such slavery, lacking the humility of Calman. But they all lose the battle; they do things against their will.

The physical journeys of Clara dominate this part of the novel. They are, as a matter of fact, more interesting than her own simple neurosis. They are described at length because Singer wants us to feel the *displacement* of things (as well as the transience of life). Space, distance, place—all are strangely dislocated and dreamlike. I am thinking especially of Clara's vision of New York. She is not prepared for it; she has been accustomed to the old world of Warsaw, Berlin, and Paris. Suddenly she sees: "In a meat market a butcher in a bloody apron sawed at a bone. Other markets and stores came into view. In their windows hung bundles of dried mushrooms, strings of garlic, cheeses bound in cloth. Everything was jumbled together: onions and oranges, radishes and apples. . . ."[49] The "jumble" is well done, suggesting that Clara notices those details which reflect her own consciousness. She projects her feelings upon the outside world.

Clara and Zipkin go to the country. (The country, as I have mentioned several times, functions as a temporary "refuge" for Singer's characters in many of the novels.) They try to make it their heaven (haven).

Ironically the country is full of coldness, rot and murky light—"all sorts of difficulties."[50] They are not at home; they leave quickly. Another exit!

Ezriel also goes on a journey to a displaced world. He visits Shaindel at the insane asylum. It is, of course, ironic that she is at home here—she has become stabilized to the routine: opium, Turkish baths, massages. There is an ambiguous tone. Questions are raised implicitly. Is Shaindel *that* mad? Is Ezriel sane? Which world (the asylum or the outside) is preferable?

Although Shaindel is insane, she perceives the instability and corruption of her husband. She sees through him. She is almost like Calman. The juxtapositions, which were quite subtle in the first part of the novel, are clear now. Shaindel and Calman are considered mad by Ezriel and Clara; they do not belong in this world. They are cast off—put away—into asylum or religious home so that they cannot interfere with the willful affairs of their respective mates. There is one important difference. Shaindel, unlike Calman, does not *choose* to retreat to a better world; *she is chosen by her demons.*

It is appropriate that after journeys to new worlds —new worlds which are not heavens after all!—Part Two ends with a "simple" exchange between Shaindel and Ezriel. Their conversation captures perfectly the metaphors of movement—escape, retreat, progress, and stasis—which are employed throughout the section (and the novel itself):

Shaindel seemed to shrink. "I sleep if they let me."
"Who doesn't?"
"They don't let me."
"Who, Shaindel, who?"
She looked at him painfully. "Leave me alone!"

"Shaindel, I'm your husband. I want to help you. I'm a
  doctor, too. Who doesn't let you sleep?"
"They don't let me—go, go away. I will be dead soon."[51]

The demons—call them "fantastic" or "real"!—do not
let her sleep. They invade heavens (as they do with
Clara and Ezriel); they make themselves at home, not
allowing humanity to be at peace. They inherit the
estate!

Part Three "resolves" tentatively the various conflicts which have been presented. Surely the most startling development is the departure of Ezriel for Israel.
(It is, of course, another journey to "a great, good
place.") Why should he leave Warsaw? His motivation is cloudy, to say the least; apparently he discovers
that he cannot stop being a Jew. He may rage against
his upbringing, his coreligionists and himself—he accepts, nevertheless, the burden that he must carry. He
becomes a kind of slave. There are several passages
which are especially relevant to Ezriel's new-found
commitment. In one we are informed that "he neither
believed in revelation nor had faith in religious traditions or dogma. Man must continually seek God. The
entire history of man was one great search for God.
But in addition man must also serve God. When he
ceased to serve God, he served tyrants. Undoubtedly
Judaism had come closest in the search for God. . . .
In the passage of two thousand years, hundreds of nations had become assimilated into other cultures. But
the Jews still struggled to return to the land of their
ancestors. This fact alone proved that the Old Testa-
ment contained divine truths."[52]

I have quoted at length because the passage is the
closest we can get to Ezriel's motivation. Notice that
he does not become an orthodox believer; he refuses to
accept divinely inspired laws. He continues to define

Jewishness as a search for divinity, a search which attempts always to battle assimilation. It is, indeed, the search (or journey) which appeals to him—not the steadfast, hermit-like enclosure. He identifies strongly with travelers (as we would expect from his various wanderings). Palestine thus becomes the ultimate frontier, and by getting there, he hopes to *begin* to believe dogma.

We do not see him at peace in Palestine. We meet him finally as a letter-writer from Switzerland. He is not joyous—as he was when he joined the Hassidic community in Marshinov—and he writes that he leaves with "a heavy heart." But he strongly affirms that he no longer has the "illusion" (or, better yet, "madness") that "our history can be obliterated. The power, whatever it is, that has kept us alive for four thousand years is still with us. I can deny God, but I cannot stop being a Jew—contradictory and strange as these words may sound."[53]

I have condemned Singer for his simplistic characterization of Ezriel. I still do. I remain unconvinced by Ezriel's "conversion"—it is neat and shocking. But even here Singer is too ironic to allow for black and white. Ezriel's letter is gray; it underlines the contradictory, strange nature of faith. *It gives and takes at the same time.* It resembles the dialectical nature of the entire novel.

Clara and Calman also undertake journeys—not to Israel but to the world after death.

Clara sees her family—father, mother, aunt, and grandparents—before she dies. She confuses time. She accepts, as does Ezriel, her history, her mortal estate. She is no longer the sick, willful woman we have known—she has fused with her background until, in death, she becomes "less and less Clara."[54] The physical details are wonderfully chosen here. "Her nose," Singer writes, "grew longer and acquired a Semitic curve, as if during her lifetime Clara had been able to keep it in check. . . . An eye opened and the pupil within looked out blindly. It was no longer Clara but a shape, a fragment of eternity."[55] Clara has at last found a resting place and, in doing so, she regains eternity. She is also a "slave" now.

After Clara dies, Calman recognizes that he must soon go. He lies in the hospital—he has moved from the manor to the religious study house and, finally, to the hospital!—and realizes without any *contradictory* feelings that he must die. He puts man in "proper perspective—a pile of bones."[56] His vision strengthens his humility: he "knew the measure of man, that he is ashes and dust."[57] Unlike Clara (who fights death until the end and loses) and Ezriel (who hopes to be reborn in Palestine), Calman *waits patiently* and prays that God will forgive his transgressions.

After the death of Clara and Calman, Ezriel travels "to what had been Calman Jacoby's estate. The sky, the cornfields, the cornflowers at the edge of the road, the birds—had all remained the same."[58] He senses that nature remains the same, but that the manor (the design of man) is transformed and often destroyed. He realizes the temporality of earthly existence, and shares his profound knowledge with us.

So we have completed another cycle. After we share Ezriel's knowledge—the rest of the novel merely echoes this moving passage—we understand that the historical novels of Singer employ ambiguous perspectives. Certainly Jews are "free" to build manors, find occupations, and construct family ties, believing that they have unlimited choice. They soon discover, however, that their freedom is ultimately restricted. Their patterns do not last: manors become corrupt; marriages break down. Then they return to their heritage. *Only by accepting enclosure as Jews, their chosen state, can they regain a sense of real freedom. Only within boundaries can they be "open."*

The open novels are full of changes—events rush past; men rise and fall (and rise?); time moves relentlessly. But the changes are fixed; they are viewed as part of a larger cycle. They incarnate "eternal return." The human events constantly suggest cosmic design. *The novels are, in a breath-taking way, open and closed!*

3

The

Closed

Novels

I believe that Singer is at his best in the closed novels (and short stories.) These are tight, claustrophobic, and concentrated—they insist upon the detailed, symbolic event, not the comprehensive sweep of history, and they consequently force us to read closely. They tend to deal with faith in an "obsessive" way because they limit themselves to an exploration of one "center of consciousness." Although they are far removed from the "all-encompassing" generational novels previously discussed, they do present the recurring themes of freedom and slavery, the nature of Jewishness.

The plots of the three closed novels are rather simple. *Satan in Goray* describes the hope for salvation (and the frustration when it does not occur). Rechele is the center of consciousness; she carries the illusions and fears of Goray within her tortured heart. Wed to Reb Itche Mates; living with Reb Gedaliya (after the departure of Reb Itche Mates); longing for quick salvation—she becomes so confused that she believes that she is impregnated by Satan, and she dies. Her fate symbolically illustrates the message that we must not seek immediate Heavens.

The Magician of Lublin presents another hero, Yasha, who is tempted to renounce his religion, wife, and magic art for the sake of Emilia, a Gentile widow. (She is not the first woman he is involved with, but she represents more of a commitment than does Magda, his Gentile assistant.) Intending to steal money to achieve his "salvation" (that is, running away with Emilia), he falls and hurts himself, and he discovers that he is wrong. He returns to his Jewish heritage, wife, and home; he accepts, as does Goray, the inadequacies of new faiths.

The Slave focuses on Jacob. He is a captive of the Poles—the time is the early 1700s—but he falls in love with Wanda. She is an Emilia-figure, although much less dignified and intelligent, who tempts him to renounce his beliefs for her paganism. He stands fast, unlike the earlier heroes, and soon discovers that she loves him so much that *she* converts. She becomes Sarah. But they learn that such "intermarriage" or conversion leads to further trouble. They are alienated from both peasants and Jews. After she dies in childbirth, Jacob flees to Palestine. The novel, however, ends with his return, death, and final burial with Sarah.

These brief descriptions alert us to the classic patterns of conversion to non-Jewish life and to eventual return. They demonstrate the underlying tensions in Singer's "preoccupied" heroes; they suggest, furthermore, that they will be symbolic, symmetrical, and claustrophobic designs.

Satan in Goray (1955) is an excellent introduction to the closed novels (as well as a fine work in itself). It begins with a lengthy description of the year 1648 in Goray. The details are historically accurate, but they seem somehow to be "mythic." Goray is "at the end of the world."[1] The wicked Ukrainians (followers of Chmelnicki)[2] sew cats inside the ripped bellies of women. Dogs tug at "dismembered limbs."[3] These details of violation are so vivid that they create an hallucinatory light. How could such massacres really happen? Are people (even in wartime) only limbs or opened bellies? By forcing us to yield to nightmare, the introductory passages unsettle our easy assumptions about reason, motivation, and reality itself.

Now Singer describes the various characters who return to Goray some years after the Chmelnicki massacre. They are not drawn in detail; they are shadows, examples, or ghosts. Rabbi Benish, who is obviously the symbol of orthodox tradition, is described only in terms of his ardent study of Torah. Rechele, the seventeen-year-old daughter of Reb Eleazar, is crippled, "mad," reclusive, and oddly sexual. Reb Mordecai Joseph, also lame, is an angry believer in the immediate coming of the Messiah (in the form of the "great and holy" Sabbatai Zevi[4]). Reb Itche Mates, a later arrival, is another firm believer in Sabbatai Zevi; he quotes homilies and parables and tries to exert power over the citizens (especially Rechele).

The town and its inhabitants are so obscurely presented that we yield to *mystery*. We cannot use modern psychological analysis to explore them—their world is dramatically beyond reason or science—and we must accept their outlines as holy text. Of course, we fight acceptance. We want to discuss Rechele's relationship to her father or her lameness as part of a clear *pattern*. We want to create our own designs (worlds). But Singer demonstrates that by yielding to such temptation we too are looking for final, clear-cut solutions; we begin to resemble the weak-minded inhabitants of Goray.

I am impressed by Singer's association of public and private worlds. He begins with a general picture of Goray—the shops, the destitute citizens, the peasants in the surrounding villages—but he soon describes the warfare in individual households: the conflict between brothers, or between fathers and sons. There is no real peace in the family and in the community at large: each person is isolated, although he apparently belongs to a greater world. Rabbi Benish banishes members of his family; Rechele hides in her room. The scene is obviously set for an "existential" situation—all the characters *stand alone*.

It is not surprising, therefore, that the "isolatoes"—

Melville's word—begin to look for some superior being (or force). They desperately seek leadership!
They desire authority! Afraid to be on their own,
especially after the holocaust, they study signs and accept "extraordinary rumors" (a chapter title). They
surrender to dreams of redemption: "Ordinary women
dreamed remarkable dreams. Dead kin told them all
about the wonders that would soon occur. Sleeping
and walking, people saw, riding an ass, that pauper
who was to be the Messiah; they heard Elijah the
Prophet call: 'Redemption cometh to the world!' "[5]
They wish to escape from freedom.

Certainly the structure of the novel (we are still
in Part One) will be an up-and-down one: despair then
hope then despair. There will not be any progression;
in a kind of manic-depressive cycle Goray will constantly alternate currents. The novel begins with a re-
port of the Chmelnicki massacre, moves to a "recon-
struction," then to more evil days of decline. Change
is rampant.

It is no wonder that the inhabitants—perhaps most
of all Rechele (whose terrifying childhood is described
at length)—want to stop time. They seek eternal order
—a "still point" which cannot change because of
whims, conflicts, and total war. They hope to live in
Heaven, not in stormy Goray.

When Reb Itche Mates arrives, carrying "holy
scripts" and promises of soon-to-be-achieved salvation,
he is eagerly welcomed. He apparently delivers answers to their situation. He divulges "mysteries of mysteries."[6] But we recognize that he is a well-meaning
"confidence man" who will supplant the weak authori-
ties which presently rule the town.

His proposal of marriage to Rechele is appropriate. He can take care of her (supplanting her weak

father); he can heal her wounds. Rechele longs to surrender to him; she has no one else to obey. She screams
at one point: "I've no strength left. Merciful God, take
me!"[7] She views Reb Itche Mates as a divine being (or
at least an emissary from the divine). The marriage is
wonderfully symbolic. Rechele is almost "Israel": torn,
indecisive, crippled, and afraid; Reb Itche is almost the
false Messiah. Their covenant is bound to be evil.

In the last chapter of Part One (before the actual
wedding takes place) we see that Rabbi Benish gives
up whatever little authority he has left. He cannot rise
from his sick bed; he surrenders to his own body (as
Rechele will continue to do in a different way), pre-
ferring to "die" rather than live in violently changing
Goray. He asks to be taken to Lublin. One woman
flings herself in front of his horses and screams: "Holy
Rabbi, why do you forsake us? Rabbi! Ho-ly Rabbi!"[8]
Rabbi Benish does not answer. There is silence now.
(The entire part has, of course, alternated between
noise and silence). With the departure of the nominal
leader (spiritual father), Goray is even more alone than
during the Chmelnicki massacre.

Part Two begins with the day of Reb Itche Mates'
wedding. He is described preparing for it by sinking to
his knees in the snow, and sitting with his feet in a
bucket of cold water. He is a man of ice—an ascetic
who shuns human heat. (He resembles some of Hawthorne's ice men.) Rechele is livid and "removed"; she
gazes into the distance. The "grotesque" qualities of
the marriage partners adds to the narrative. So does
their incomplete wedding night. They remain locked
in their private dreams; they pervert the traditional
ritual. The horror which has been slowly developing
(and has reached a high point with the Rabbi's departure) is even stronger. Sterility exists at home and,

by symbolic extension, in Jewish Goray. We are informed that even after "the seventh day of the Seven
Days of the Marriage Feast was passed, Rechele was
still a virgin. . . . Everyone believed that sorcery had
prevented the bride and groom from consummating
their marriage."[9]

Reb Gedaliya arrives in the midst of this despair,
sterility, and wonder-seeking. He is another emissary,
bringing good news from the outside world. (Singer
always reminds us that Goray, like its inhabitants, is
isolated and, consequently, dependent upon others.)
He is robust, tall, and powerful—"an individual of
standing"[10]—and his physical appearance immediately
suggests that unlike all the victims we have met (Reb
Itche Mates, Rechele, and Rabbi Benish), he can *take
control* of the situation. *He masters it*: "Life seemed to
have become more pleasant in Goray with Reb Gedaliya's appearance. Despite the frost, the day was sun-
filled. The snowy hills around Goray reflected sunlight,
blinding the eyes, and miraculously blending earth
with sky. The air smelled of Passover, of salvation, and
of consolation."[11] The passage bears close reading. Reb
Gedaliya is surely a wonder-maker; he brings changes
in nature. He charges the atmosphere with light. But
his power is more apparent than real—note the words
"seemed," "blinded the eyes." It is given to him by
Goray's citizens, who want such dazzling signs. Perhaps the most significant word is "blended" (interestingly paired with "blinded")—*by adopting Reb
Gedaliya, they almost fuse with him, neglecting all
meaningful separations and hierarchies.*

Singer alerts us to the dangers of communism. Reb
Gedaliya and his followers refuse to view life in proper
perspective. They neglect boundaries, laws, levels. Men
and women sit together during the services; they

mingle, "like one family." (We remember the typical conflicts in Singer's fictional families.) It is not surprising that Reb Gedaliya and Rechele are "wed" after Reb Itche Mates goes on a journey to seek Sabbatai Zevi—"he lived with her under one roof although she was a matron."[12] The roles of "leader," "wife," "virgin," among others, have lost all meaning. Everything is permitted!

The "blending" is carefully described to suggest the utter corruption of Goray. Several passages come to mind: "Once two wandering beggars who had come to Goray decided to marry, and married they were by some mischief makers on a dung-hill."[13] The commandment against adultery is annulled. Incest occurs. Voyeurism goes unchecked. Reb Gedaliya lies with Rechele—his robust frame joins her white, semi-transparent body—and proclaims that "this is the hour of union":[14] "The Divine Parents are coupling face to face."[15]

The pace of the novel accelerates. Goray is not content to see just one "miracle." It wants more and more—a *climactic event*. (The sexual associations are probably valid here because Singer dwells so much upon the blending of sexuality and religion. It is difficult to determine how much he condemns this kind of blending.) It hopes for the Ultimate Day: "according to all calculations this was the day on which the great blast was to be heard. But the sun set—and nothing had occurred."[16]

"But the sun set—and nothing had occurred." The sentence bears repeating. When the inhabitants realize that the sun will continue to set—there will not be eternal light just now!—despite the prayers, hopes, and "wonders" generated by Reb Gedaliya, they plunge into despair. They recognize the existence of limits:

"The people of Goray fell asleep in their clothes, their mouths open and their hearts hollow. . . ."[17] They even begin to look more closely at Reb Gedaliya, no longer blinded by his seeming wonders.

The wheel turns once again. Now warfare erupts in Goray; civil strife destroys the previous semblance of unity, hope-giving communion. This conflict is perhaps more terrifying than the Chmelnicki massacre because *Jews are hurting Jews*. Sects battle each other: "The Sabbatai Zevi hurled themselves murderously at their opponents, whom they beat and trampled underfoot, ruining their clothes and prayer shawls."[18] Further breakdown is captured vividly when Singer describes a "fault" in the prayer-house wall, extending "from the roof to the foundation. . . ."[19] The entire structure is cracked!

With the return of Reb Mordecai Joseph and Reb Itche Mates from their quest of Sabbatai Zevi, the downward swing becomes even more violent. We recall the earlier golden emissaries, and like the Goray inhabitants we are shocked at these new ones. The abject appearance of both men causes universal distress; they have grasped the truth. Sabbatai Zevi is not the Messiah; no Messiah will rescue them from their bloody civil war. We are told that "all of the congregation bowed their shoulders, as under a heavy burden. They looked exactly as they had that day in the year 1648 when messengers brought them the evil news that Cossacks and Tartars encircled Goray."[20] Now we recognize the function of the repeated arrivals (and departures). *History repeats itself! There is no way to stop the flow of events, to stabilize life—Goray cannot have eternal union on this earth*. The attempt to escape from human pain and struggle—to obey the promises of Sabbatai Zevi (or his representative, Reb Gedaliya)—

must ultimately lead to perversion, corruption, and despair.

But the faithful believers in Sabbatai Zevi cannot let go of their once-powerful reign. They try to give the townsfolk the license to do *anything*; in this way they can still control the situation. Satan dances in the street. Goray becomes an "accursed town."[21] The Lord's name is "everywhere desecrated."[22]

It is the detailed progression which creates the power of the novel (especially after the arrival of Reb Gedaliya). Singer does not merely state the universal implications of his parable; he delights in giving us "all the facts." I am strongly impressed by his chapters, "The Sacred and the Profane" and "Rechele Is Impregnated by Satan." Suddenly Rechele is again the center of attention; her body and mind are the stage. (Reb Gedaliya and the Faithful function only in relation to her.)

She is the suffering, half-crazy "vessel": her "skull seemed to be filled with sand, her mouth was agape . . . Her throat was narrow and swollen, almost strangled; her congealed blood slowly warmed and began to flow again through her veins. It would seem to Rechele that her body had actually died and gradually was reviving."[23] Her agonies—and there are more to come!—are wonderfully exact; they are, indeed, more alive than her earlier prophecies. They are also symbolic. Rechele is torn by disputation between the sacred and profane; she writhes, as do the Goray inhabitants (and the Jews in general), because she cannot give herself willingly to one or the other. (She incarnates the up-and-down cycle of the entire novel.) Finally she is raped by the profane in the shape of the "Thing": "He threw her down, and entered her. She cried a bitter cry, but there was no sound, and she started from sleep."²⁴ She wakes and loses her identity—she is merely another *thing*.

Rechele sinks; so does Goray. Both are, ironically enough, married to Satan because they have surrendered their true faith. Trying to rise, they fall into the abyss. They suffer the consequences of their ill-formed covenant.

The novel should end here because there is a sense of finality. Singer, unfortunately, cannot accept such enclosure; he believes that things will improve, that hope prevails. He gives us two final chapters which are written "at a distance." Rechele and Goray are put into perspective by a scribe so that their lessons can be taught to others who would, like them, seek the Messiah. Although Singer frames the detailed progression by his startling method, he sacrifices the power the narrative has accumulated. "Real" agonies are objectified and lost.

There is great irony here. Throughout the novel Singer has demonstrated that men should not attempt to stop the flow of time (and live in Heaven on Earth). Now he allows the flow to continue—the scribe writes after the death of Rechele—and, by doing so, he perverts the fictional design. He murders his creation for the sake of hope! He is, strangely, guilty of the same drive for Messianic salvation as the Goray inhabitants. Perhaps I am too literary here. I understand that Singer wants to give us a hopeful moral—"*The Messiah will come in God's own time*"²⁵—but his moral reduces the breathtaking power of blackness he has artfully established. His own ambivalence, which should have been understood and mastered, creates the unhappy "final solution."

The Magician of Lublin (1960) is, like most of

Singer's fictions, precisely titled. Although Yasha Ma-
zur is his real name, his ability as a magician is the most
important thing about him. He is linked with the ability to "defy" natural law (or, at least, to make believe
that he can). His calling is highly symbolic. He is the
master of rebellion, the supreme trickster, the miracle-
man. "No one could duplicate his skill. He would be
imprisoned in a room at night with the lock clamped
on the outside of the door, and the next morning he
would be seen nonchalantly strolling through the
market place, while on the outside of the door the lock
remained unopened."[26] Note the careful details. The
magician defies imprisonment—his fascination with
locks is stressed throughout his adventures—and gains
freedom mysteriously. The ironies begin. He can do
this trick only as a "performer" on stage. When he attempts to free himself in his daily life, he is not as
successful.

The magician is caught. Although he considers
himself "half Jew, half Gentile—neither Jew nor Gentile,"[27] he cannot completely unlock his Jewish heritage. He continues to believe in God. He continues to
brood about the prayer-house. He passes one and
realizes that "it was all strangely foreign to him, yet
familiar . . . He, Yasha, chose to remain a moment
longer. He was part of this community. Its roots were
his roots. He bore its marks upon his flesh. . . ."[28] He
resembles Ezriel and the narrator of *In My Father's
Court* in his entangling ambivalence.

The magician is also caught by passion. He cannot stop pursuing women; he loves many at one time
because he shuns formal commitment. But at the same
time, he feels oddly bound to his wife, Esther. Marriage—or any lasting relationship—inhibits his freedom.
Singer is, as usual, describing the imprisonment of self-

love which destroys marriage, but he is perhaps more successful in presenting it here than in his comprehensive novels. We really understand why the magician feels threatened.

Passion and religion—the two forces are united in his affair with Emilia. She is Catholic; she demands that he marry her and convert to her faith. "He had to decide this very night, choose between his religion and the cross, between Esther [his Jewish wife] and Emilia, between honesty and crime (a single crime for which, with God's help, he would later make restitution). But his mind would resolve nothing. Instead of attacking the main problem, it dallied, went off on tangents, became frivolous."[29]

The magician wants to rise above decision-making. Even before he travels to Warsaw for his "act," he dreams "that he was flying. He rose above the ground and soared, soared. He wondered why he had not tried it before—it was so easy, so easy. He dreamt this almost every night, and each time awoke with the sensation that a distorted kind of reality had been revealed to him."[30] He decides that he can fly in his act and, more important, that he can transcend human commitments.

I underline his movement because throughout the novel it is employed symbolically. We first meet the magician at home, resting in bed. He is peaceful with Esther. But as soon as the holiday—which interestingly enough, coincides with a Jewish holy day—is concluded, he must take to the road. He travels to Warsaw for his performance; he is, in fact, known there as "The Magician," not as Yasha. Ironically, the closer he gets to Warsaw (where Emilia lives) and the farther from home, the more static and immobile he becomes. Is he free resting at home? Is he free on the road? Is he free in the "new" world of Warsaw? He cannot answer these questions. *Perhaps he longs to fly above each of these places.*

In the first third of the novel (up to the arrival in Warsaw and the first visit to Emilia) there is growing suspense generated by the tension between the magician's aspirations (his "openness") and possible enclosures. The tension makes this "closed" novel, which insists upon narrowing the focus to his spiritual choice, even more dramatic than *Satan in Goray*. The earlier novel stressed the enclosure of the town (symbolically standing for all Jews); here the enclosure is centered upon the magician's consciousness. He is, indeed, a much more interesting personality than Rechele (also trapped) or, for that matter, Clara and Ezriel in the historical novels. *His actions are married to the structure of the novel; both are curiously tight, obsessive, locked.*

The novel tightens even more. The magician knows that he must gain money before he can marry Emilia (and offer a cash settlement to his wife). But how? The only way is by stealing. Gradually he drifts into believing that he can utilize his "flying" talent and climb into the apartment of wealthy people. The irony is clear (almost too clear!). His private world is no longer the same. He flies *for someone else*; he is enclosed even as he "ascends." He is quite ready for a fall!

The ascent and fall are vividly described (so that we enjoy the physical details while we understand their symbolic value): "The impossible was really so possible. Opening the French doors proved more difficult; they were locked from the inside. But he tugged violently on the door and lifted the chain with the skeleton key which he always carried on his person."[31]

The magician tries to become his act. He discovers, however, that he cannot perform naturally. He broods; he questions his movements; he fumbles. Thus he cannot do his usual tricks. He cannot unlock the safe: the lock "was like a child's puzzle, which if not solved at once eludes one for hours. He needed an instrument that could reach to the lock's vitals."[32] His skill is lost. He panics. He loses his self-control (necessary for tricks), blaming his misfortune on "a dybbuk, a satan, an implacable adversary who would disconnect while he was juggling, push him from the tightrope, make him impotent."[33] (The associations here are interesting —somehow the flying talent is related to sexual ability. But why does he think of sexuality at this point?)

Now he flees. He steps onto the balcony. His feet "lacked their usual sureness. He wished to support them upon the shoulders of a statue but they fell short of the goal. For a moment he hung from the edge of the balcony feeling that he was about to doze off— suspended in air. But then he wedged his foot in a depression in the wall."[34] The details are artfully presented. The magician cannot control his body (his feet or his heart). He tries to find support from some stronger being (represented by the statue), but he is on his own. He dangles in air; then he hits the wall. It is the wall which, like a locked door, encloses him. He hurts his foot, and his injury symbolically maims him, preventing the continued use of his talent. He is impotent; *he is no longer the magician!*

It is only after the loss of his miraculous ability that he converts. He "runs" away from the apartment house and hides in a synagogue. (Symbolically he finds shelter; he does not need to break into the place.) He now performs as a believer, putting on the prayer shawl and phylacteries, and intoning the prayers in

Hebrew. Soon he forgets that he is faking things; he begins to believe the words: "For years he had shunned the synagogues. All of a sudden, in the course of days, he had twice strayed into houses of worship. . . ."[35] He humbly admits: "I must be a Jew! . . . . A Jew like all the others!"[36] The magician, or, better yet, Yasha finds a new calling, perhaps recognizing that there is after all, only one Miracle Worker.

Yasha must still answer questions: Can he marry Emilia without money? Can he give up this new-won faith? He visits her, hoping to clarify matters by admitting his guilt, and by sharing his secrets. He wants to join others (to perform as part of a team). How difficult! He learns that although he is merely another human being, he remains isolated. He is ridiculed by Emilia; he cannot convince her. He finally recognizes the truth of her statement: "Possibly you've crippled yourself for life. You must have some sort of covenant with God since he punished you directly on the spot."[37] *He does have his own covenant with God; he cannot share it with anyone else.* He is still on his own (as far as other people are concerned). He can perform only for God.

But there are still turns in the road for Yasha. He must make peace with Magda (his assistant and mistress) and his wife. He cannot forsake them; yet he cannot really live with them. He has to decide and act, but he is powerless: "He trembled all over. His fingers had become white and shrunken, the tips shriveled like those of a mortally-ill person, or of a corpse."[38]

He goes, at last, to tell Magda and discovers that she has killed herself. She hangs "from the ceiling, an overturned chair beneath her."[39] (Her death is symbolically related to the motif of movement. She dangles, as did Yasha before he gave himself to his religion, and her lifeless movement appropriately suggests his former life.) He feels guilty, realizing that for every commitment—as in this case his need to give up his assistant (and his talent itself)—there is destruction. Indeed, this is the tightrope: we walk between two stations; once we move toward one, we, of course, relinquish the other. And we must keep moving; we cannot merely suspend ourselves in midair. Yasha seeks seclusion now, and he gives up the noise of the street. He wants to be a performer for God, and he totally abandons his magician act. It is appropriate that he believes that "the last twenty-four hours were unlike any previous day he had experienced. They summed up all his previous existence, and in summing it up had put a seal upon it. He had seen the hand of God. He had reached the end of the road."[40]

The epilogue, like the concluding chapters of *Satan in Goray*, tries to "frame" Yasha, to seal his destiny. I think that it succeeds because it does not really shock us. He becomes a Penitent, living in a small brick structure in the courtyard of his house. (Three years have passed.) "A few bricks removed and he could—he knew—wriggle through the window. But the thought that he could fight his way to freedom at any moment he chose stifled his desire to live in his cell."[41] He commits himself to a final resting place; he no longer wants to be on the road (as he did at the beginning of the novel) or, for that matter, to fly above his kind.

Although I am not surprised by Yasha's decision —he is, after all, as "obsessive" here as he was about his magic talent—I am disturbed by the ease of his new performance. It is true that his faith wavers in his prison—that he sometimes goes to the edge of madness as he disputes his past with himself—but he nevertheless

manages to remain unconvincing. He is manipulated
by Singer (and we, in turn, are manipulated by both
of them). Perhaps there is intended irony. Are we
supposed to condemn his seclusion? Doesn't he neglect
others (as he did before) for the sake of his religious
performance? Consider the thought: "One could not
serve God amongst other men even though separated
by brick walls."[42] Yasha is denying the relevance of
humanity; he is attempting to play God—to be a Messiah. He is almost like the villains of Goray, who
neglected the town for some higher purpose. I am unsure about Singer's view of his hero. It seems to me
that it is somewhat ambivalent.

It is revealing that Yasha does not entirely remove himself from other men. He looks with love at
Esther when she brings him food. He listens to her
gossip. In this respect he goes against the bleak thought
which I have just discussed. He is self-contradictory.
This quality not only demonstrates that he still needs
an audience—Esther is a spectator of his actions (at
least part of the time)—but it also humanizes him again.
*Yasha is neither Penitent nor Magician—he is not bound
by titles.* He is what he is (or does). He moves beyond
abstractions.

So does Singer. He concludes the novel with a
letter sent to Yasha by "eternally devoted Emilia."[43]
She writes of her recent marriage to Professor Ryd-
zewski, her memories of their past, and her hopes. Two
sentences are especially important: "In my fantasies I
always pictured you in America in a huge theater or
circus, surrounded by luxury and beautiful women.
But reality is full of surprises."[44] Emilia, like Yasha,
admits that because reality is so surprising, it inhibits
our freedom—we can function only within the limits
of surprise. Not knowing what will come next, or

what our audience looks like, we must somehow commit ourselves and perform "naturally." How magical
if we succeed! Emilia and Yasha share this hard-earned
knowledge. We admire their wisdom.

The Slave (1962) is a dialectically structured
novel. It contains three parts—we remember the three-
part structure of *The Manor* and *The Estate*—which
exist in creative tension and "resolution." But the
structure is not literary or artificial; it never destroys
the resonance of this love story.

The novel begins with these sentences: "A single
bird call began the day. Each day the same bird, the
same call. It was as if the bird signaled the approach
of dawn to its brood. Jacob opened his eyes."[45] There
is a sense of "eternal return"—each day the same actions occur: the bird calls Jacob to rise and greet the
beginning of things. Man and nature are in harmony;
each is married to the other. There is emphasis upon
vision—the opening of eyes, the receptivity to environ-
ment, and the unity of "self" and "other." I maintain
that these opening sentences give us the key to the
novel.

Jacob is a slave of Polish peasants; he has been
captured after a massacre of Jews. The time is the
seventeenth century, but as the introductory passage
indicates—and as most of Singer's fictions insist—the
time is eternal: *before or after holocaust.* (Think of
The Family Moskat, The Estate or *Satan in Goray*.)
He is not aware of the *precise* day or hour; he can tell
time only in relation to the birds or the light. He is, on
the surface, without roots. But as we continue reading, we realize that he is rooted in Jewish words. He
says his "prayers by heart, a few chapters of the Mishnah, some pages of the Gemarah, a host of Psalms, as

well as passages from various parts of the Bible."[46] He
regards his survival—and the survival of Jewish words
in his mind—as living proof of cosmic design. He believes, consequently, in miracles: "Every sunrise in
the mountains was like a miracle; one clearly discerned
God's hand among the flaming clouds."[47]

Jacob is a "slave"; he obeys in a humble (yet
strong) manner the commands of his master. He lacks
the dramatic self-confidence of Yasha or, in a different
way, of Reb Gedaliya. But even he finds that "slavery"
is not a simple matter. He is also enslaved to Wanda,
the daughter of his Polish master, and this enslave-
ment—shall we call it love?—conflicts with his Jewish
heritage. Even he must make a decision between kinds
of slavery. (It is one decision which resembles that of
Yasha—between love of a Gentile woman and love of
God.) Jacob tends to avoid making the decision. He
proclaims that he cannot love Wanda: *it is forbidden.*

But as the first part of the novel continues, Jacob
loses the sense of "openness" he had at sunrise. He begins to be at war with himself. He understands the
growing sense of enclosure. When harvest time ap-
proaches, he is compelled to come down from the
mountain and join the peasants: "How painful it was
for the slave to leave his solitude."[48] He sees further
signs of his conflict-torn entrapment.

Singer gives us detailed descriptions of ceremonies and events—indeed, all events are viewed as sacred
ceremonies!—which help us to understand Jacob's
condition. We view Jacob sitting "midway between
the barn and rock, concealing himself with weeds and
the branches of a midget pine. He mined within himself as men dig for treasure in the earth. It was slow
work; he scratched sentences, fragments of sentences,
single words into the stone. The Torah had not dis-

appeared. It lay hidden in the nooks and crannies of his brain."[49] The entire passage is fascinating. He sits "midway"—he is the man between things (freedom and slavery, Jew and Gentile). He must decide on his own; he must uncover his buried life. But he is in a pit himself under "weeds." The stress is upon enclosure, but enclosure is not bleak. It is, in fact, a buried treasure. Jacob knows also that although he is "midway" and "alone," he is, nevertheless, related to other Jews. He is part of a tradition which lies hidden in his consciousness. He must unearth it.

Jacob watches a Polish ritual. He stares at a straw effigy of a Baba, a goddess, which is thrown into a stream. The peasants hope that she takes with her "the evil eye and all their misfortunes and illnesses."[50] Jacob is amused by the pagan ritual. We realize, however, that he is also "drowning" in a sea of bad spirits and that he needs divine purification. He must seek clear water.

The details of dirt and cleanliness are reinforced throughout this first part. Jacob finds, for example, that enclosure clouds his vision. He looks at the sky: "No longer was there a vista of distant places—nothing was visible but the flat crest of the hill surrounding the barn. . . . Here in his exile Jacob at last understood what was meant when the cabala spoke of God's hidden face and the shrinking of His light. Yesterday everything had been bright; now it was gray. . . . If so much could vanish for the physical eyes, how much more could elude the spiritual. Every man comprehended according to his merit."[51] Jacob wants to recapture purity, distance, and elevation. But he is dirtied by fog *and* impurities of self. He believes that he does not merit "infinite worlds, angels. . . ."[52] He regards himself as "immersed in the vanities of the body."[53] How to rise? How to see? How to gain free-dom? The physical details and spiritual meanings puz-zle him, but he at least recognizes that they are one.

Jacob's dilemma—he, like Yasha, walks a tight-rope—is greater when he realizes the nature of his en-slavement to Wanda. He needs her so much that he goes against the Law. He expresses his love. When Wanda says that she has no one but him, the effect is double-edged. This is Singer's wish. He makes us un-derstand that for every love (commitment), there is a counterforce. One slavery violates another slavery.

It is even more ironic that after Jacob is released from slavery—he is purchased by the Jews of his home town—he cannot accept his old way of life. He is, in-deed, so unhappy that he sits in the study house and whispers to God: "it is impossible for me to obey the commandment, Thou Shalt Love Thy God. No, I cannot, Father, not in this life."[54] He blames God for his present condition (and the massacres of the Jews). He looks with disgust at his coreligionists breaking "the code regulating man's treatment of man."[55] His former humility has given way to self-love.

Jacob decides to return to Wanda. He rediscov-ers the beauty of the countryside: "How beautiful the countryside was and how contrary to his despair. . . . If only I could live in perpetual summer and do harm to no one, he murmured, as the wagon entered a pine wood which seemed less a forest than some heavenly mansion."[56] He finds the natural scene appealing be-cause it is "removed"; it promises solitude and non-slavery: "All of these creatures knew what was ex-pected of them. None sought to rebel against its Creator. Man alone acted viciously."[57] Jacob's vision encompasses light (even after he closes his eyes, blinded as he is by so much splendor): "A roseate light seeped through his lids. Gold mingled with blue, green with purple, and out of this whirlpool of color, Wanda's image formed."[58] Wanda is the center of his vision.

They meet at last (as Part One ends). They are not the "equals" we want them to be; they still are different. Jacob regards Wanda as a potential Jew—a "future daughter of Israel."[59] By converting her to the faith he has never really left, he can solve the painful dilemma. He can possess the two worlds of "slavery." Wanda apparently agrees with him although she claims that his return is the result of witchcraft, not free will: "I made a clay image of you and I wrapped it in my hair. I bought an egg laid by a black hen and buried it at the crossroads with a piece of glass from a broken mirror. I looked into it and I saw your eyes. . . ."[60] (Note how Singer returns again to the symbolic details of dirt, burial, and vision—these make her simple declaration reverberate with accumulated meaning.) They kiss and shudder.

Part Two begins with "a time of upheaval."[61] The social instability is described at length to make us aware again of various forms of injustice and slavery. The Jews are *survivors*, remembering and hoping for better times. In the town of Pilitz arrive a couple, Jacob and Sarah. Sarah is really Wanda who, by adopting a new name, has begun her "conversion" to Judaism. She is a "mute" so that she won't have to admit her Gentile origins. Jacob is still her teacher—and the new teacher of the community. Their love stands in sharp contrast to the general violence around them.

There is further emphasis upon "miracle." (In Part One we remember Jacob regarding the natural scene as evidence of God's miraculous power.) Sarah unwittingly speaks to Adam Pilitzsky, the Gentile lord of the manor, as she defends her husband. (She calls Jacob a "holy man."[62] Her words are taken as divinely inspired. They shock everyone. Why should Singer make so much of the words? Are they merely introduced for the sake of the plot? I think that once more he employs the sudden vision. *Sarah's words, spoken out of desperation, somehow get to the essence of Jacob—they echo our sentiments.* They are miraculous because they bind us to her (and her husband). They offer the shocks of recognition and love.

Jacob is now regarded as a "saint" or miracle-worker, but he knows even more than previously, that his power is limited. He cannot fathom events and people; he cannot read things at all: "Itself a cabalistic book, the night was crowded with sacred names and symbols—mystery upon mystery. . . . The stars looked like letters of the alphabet, vowel points, notes of music. . . . The world was a parchment scrawled with words and song."[63] Jacob regards the universe as holy text filled with miraculous letters of the alphabet. He tries to be a faithful, devoted reader (and interpreter). By linking world and letter, he is, of course, linking literature to religion in much the same way Singer does constantly in his fictions. He is, in this respect, a counterpart of the author. The passage reveals another reason for the stress upon Sarah's muteness (and "subsequent" speech)—throughout the novel words and visions are wed. The implication is that although holiness must occur spontaneously, it can be described only with carefully chosen words. The novel is then about itself as holy text!

Singer presents the scene of Sarah's labor—she gives birth to a son—in terms of the symbolism I have been charting. She wails; she claims that she is Wanda; she reveals by her speech patterns that she is a Gentile.

Her words are again "miraculous"—at least initially—but after much thought the Jewish community understands that she is not a saint. Her very words are used against her!

Singer writes that "I will say nothing, Jacob decided. Now that she is speaking I must be still. He stood, lips tightly sealed, determined to endure his tribulations to the end. . . . Prayer alone was left to him but his lips refused to open even to prayer."[64] Jacob finds himself in Sarah's former condition; he acts as a "mute," realizing that although words can be holy, they can also be destructive if misinterpreted by others. He chooses silence as a kind of rebellion—not only against his fellow Jews but also against God. He will not accept future slavery.

The wonderful juxtapositions of silence and speech continue. Sarah sings "in a half yodel, half sob."[65] Her song indicates her *divided* nature. The baby cries loudly (and is not circumcised because he is a Gentile like his mother). Jacob speaks gently to her as he watches her condition worsen. He reads her silent lips: "her chapped lips seemed to say I've passed through everything."[66] Finally she dies. His last words to her are "Holy soul."[67]

Jacob is alone once more. Exiled from the Jewish community for "marrying" a Gentile (and fathering a Gentile boy), he takes his son and leaves Poland.

Part Two ends with two significant symbolic passages. Jacob finds himself in a forest. He sees a "strange light":[68] "the trunks of the pine trees seemed aflame. Far off in a clearing between the trees he saw a conflagration. A moment later, he realized it was the sun."[69] He is the visionary again. He is the man of light in harmony with the natural, holy flame. (We remember the sunrise of the first sentences.) In the midst of such "luminosity," he recognizes that darkness is "only a bad dream."[70]

The other passage involves the holiness of words. Jacob names his son "Benjamin" because the name links the baby with the first, biblical Benjamin (a name meaning child born of sorrow). He believes that the name carries on the *tradition*. And he sees now that like his own namesake, he too has lost a beloved wife, crossed a river, and been pursued by another Esau. The recurring name (be it Jacob or Benjamin) shines as a guiding light: "Everything remained the same: the ancient love, the ancient grief. Perhaps four thousand years would again pass; somewhere, at another river, another Jacob would walk mourning another Rachel."[71]

Jacob recognizes the timelessness of his name and condition. He shares his fate with others; he is bound to them. He accepts his "slavery" to history and to God. Thus he says silently: "Lead, God, lead. It is thy world."[72]

Part Three, entitled "The Return," is the shortest section in the novel. It resolves the tensions between self and community, Jew and Gentile, freedom and slavery, which have been presented.

It begins twenty years after the events in Part Two. Although we read of a time of upheaval—the lord of Pilitz has killed himself; the Jews have recognized the falseness of Sabbatai Zevi; the city has grown; the cemetery has spread "to the spot where Sarah lay"[73]—the time is recorded as dim past. *Now there is a sense of proper order, of wounds healed, of timeless design.* Thus this novel, like *Satan in Goray* and *The Magician of Lublin*, ends with a frame effect. Characters and events are enclosed.

When we again meet Jacob, we are shocked because he is described "at a distance." He is a "tall, white-bearded man, in a white gabardine and white hat, sandals on his bare feet. . . ."[74] He does not look like a Polish Jew but like an emissary from the Holy Land. He is almost a mythic stranger here—a wandering Jew—because we do not know his motives in returning to Pilitz. This new role is, of course, wonderfully appropriate; it enhances the suggestions of timelessness given at the end of Part Two (when Jacob remembers his namesake).

We, like the townsfolk, study him and gradually learn his reasons for return. He wants to bury Sarah— she is no longer referred to as Gentile Wanda—and find a resting place next to her. He wants to be "married" in death, preferably in the Holy Land. He is sustained—and has been sustained the past twenty years! —by the thought of peaceful enclosure. I want to stress the idea of peaceful enclosure. Like the scribe who describes the end of Rechele in *Satan in Goray* and Yasha the Penitent who encloses himself in the cell, Jacob seeks an end to wandering, a final shelter. He is more believable here than Yasha because he has always been confined, enslaved; he has accepted it as perfectly natural—not very threatening.

The enclosure theme is strongly advanced by the symbols in this part (even more so than the references to "buried treasure" earlier in the novel). He sits in the study house, knowing that he cannot return to the Holy Land. Then he lies in the poorhouse. He cannot move after he wakes: "His wish had always been to die in the shadow of the holy ruins, near the graves of saints, surrounded by cabalists and ascetics, and to be buried on the Mount of Olives. . . . Yet it was fortunate that he had the foresight to carry with him a small bag of earth from the Holy Land."[75] He man-

ages to move once more to the study house. Here he
thinks that there is already "an impenetrable wall"[76]
between him and his visitors. He looks at his body as
a prison. His death agony begins: his "dark cabin with
its rags and refuse was left behind on the ship."[77] After
the references to earth, wall, grave, shelter—all of
which make the account of his death vividly claustrophobic—we have the final enclosure at the end of the
journey: "He, Jacob, had arrived."[78]

Jacob is free at last after death. (Slavery is mortality.) The miracle occurs: the townsfolk discover
the remains of Sarah lying next to Jacob's soon-to-be-
filled grave: "All saw the hand of Providence in this
event. It was like one of the ancient miracles, a sign
that there is an Eye which sees and a scale wherein
even the acts of the stranger are weighed."[79] They are
"converted" by this vision—the novel continues to
insist upon (in)sight—and they chisel a stone with
"two doves facing each other, their beaks joined in a
kiss."[80] (We remember the single bird mentioned in
the opening sentences; Jacob and Sarah have become
two doves or, better yet, one bird as a result of the
kiss.)

The last paragraph of the novel reminds us of the
holiness of words, the eternal return incarnated in language: "The epitaph was completed by a passage from
the Bible encircling their names: 'Lovely and pleasant
in their lives, and in their death they were not divided.' "[81] Jacob and Sarah are viewed finally as "encircled" by the Bible; they have played parts in a holy
pattern (text) which recurs from generation to generation. The paragraph is finally not only about completed circles; it is, in fact, a completed circle itself
because it fulfills the potentialities of the entire novel.

4

The

Short

Stories

Singer is perhaps more effective as a short story writer than as a novelist. By narrowing his focus even more than he does in the closed novels, he can concentrate upon the intense vision of details. He can give us dream, stylization, and parable.

Gimpel the Fool (1957) is his first collection of stories. Like the other collections which follow, it contains at least a few stories which are masterpieces and deserve close study. I will concentrate on these, hoping thereby to suggest his complete artistic strength.

The title story is probably his finest achievement here (and among all the collections). It is narrated by Gimpel, who promptly labels himself a "fool" because other people call him this name. Is he "foolish"? The question is posed immediately; it is at the heart as what follows. Singer thus tightens the story to include one theme—the nature of "foolishness."

It is a large one, involving the meanings we assign to "belief." Gimpel disagrees with the community's label—he is another Singer rebel—but he goes along with it. He understands social needs. He does more—he realizes (dimly?) that all things are possible. *Maybe* he is a fool; *maybe* the others are: "In the first place, everything is possible. . . ."[1]

Gimpel cannot function in the "real" world (involving marriage, adultery, children) because he assumes wrongly that others will act with faith. He cannot understand deceitfulness. He thinks positively. When he sees his wife in bed with another man, he believes that he may be dreaming: "Hallucinations do happen. You see a figure or a mannikin or something,

70

but when you come up closer it's nothing, there's not a thing there."[2] He is constantly dreaming.

But the ironies persist. Gimpel is an absolutist; he believes that if one wavers in his acceptance of events and character, he loses sight of the design: "However, I resolved that I would always believe what I was told. What's the good of *not* believing? Today it's your wife you don't believe; tomorrow it's God Himself you won't take stock in."[3] Of course, he is foolish in such statements. Or is he? We have seen in other Singer fictions what occurs when people become relativists, wavering in their judgment. They are tortured, divided by doubts. They begin to believe absolutely in non-belief—as does Asa Bannet or Ezriel —and they reach the same point finally (from the other side of belief) as does simple-minded Gimpel.

Gimpel cannot stay at home. He leaves Frampol, his town, and goes into the world. He grows old and white. He hears many stories but he still accepts the "eternal return." (Think of Jacob in *The Slave*.) He says: "Whatever doesn't really happen is dreamed at night. It happens to one if it doesn't happen to another, tomorrow if not today, or a century hence if not next year."[4]

He is beyond "time" because he is beyond "reality." He becomes more and more shadowy; he marries his dreams: "No doubt the world is entirely an imaginary world, but it is only once removed from the true world."[5] He believes that he will see the truth only after death—then the world he enters "will be real, without complication, without ridicule, without deception."[6] How silly! How profound!

"Gimpel the Fool" is written in such a way as to reinforce the ironies of the hero. It is narrated as a series of folk happenings; it rambles; it stays on the surface of things. But its simplicity (which mirrors Gimpel's foolishness) is more apparent than real. Details are carefully chosen to suggest the ambiguities of belief. I have already mentioned the contrariness of the opening. Look closely at these lines: "I am Gimpel the Fool. I don't think myself a fool. On the contrary. But that's what folks call me."[7] These simple sentences deal with difficult philosophical (religious) positions. Gimpel asserts that he is Gimpel the Fool; he knows, at least in the first sentence, that his identity is clearly reflected in his name. He exists "foolishly." But the second sentence affirms that he is *not* foolish—that his identity exists somewhere else, that it has no relation to his name. *He is not what he is.* (He again recalls Jacob, who also became fascinated with names.) He is a man of contraries. His identity—his very existence—dwells in some other, non-social reality; it belongs to the Lord. Gimpel lives in a "real" world, not Frampol, in which names (language itself) are not needed.

In the last sentences of the story, he says: "God be praised: there [the real world] even Gimpel cannot be deceived."[8] I take these to mean that he can know himself truly only when he knows God truly. Now he can only hope and praise, losing his identity in such celebration. He has solved his contrariness (of the opening lines) by growing in his faith. Or has he discovered the faith which he has always possessed? Is the story progressive or cyclical? I am not sure, but even this uncertainty is part of Singer's design—his artistic attempt to pervert our rational, needlessly complex (or simple) explications.

"The Gentleman from Cracow" is another kind of story. It begins with a lengthy description of Frampol —a village which lies "amid thick forests and deep swamps."⁹ Poverty reigns; "gold coin" is rarely seen. Obviously the description, although it is not narrated by the hero as in "Gimpel the Fool," tries to establish a mythic sense. The forests, the swamps, the faded chronicle, the absence of gold—all these elements recur in dreams and folk narratives. (They echo the ones in *Satan in Goray*.)

In Frampol "miracles" can happen. Thus a stranger (again an "emissary") arrives one day in the midst of a locust-filled, dry summer. He is said to be a "gift from heaven";¹⁰ he bears good tidings and alms. We, like the townsfolk, are tempted to believe in his wonders—to accept the signs. The story is one of false belief or, better yet, belief in falseness. It apparently contradicts "Gimpel the Fool" because it suggests that we should not believe absolutely—we must discern shadows, doubts, and divisions.

We recognize our "foolishness"—surely a different kind from Gimpel's—as we observe a game of cards. There is too much good luck—the "gleam" of gold coin is excessively bright. Something is wrong! Our fears increase as the gentleman suggests that there should be a "ball" during which he will choose a wife. His dark motives are unclear—he is a dream-like figure who is, we shall see, beyond human outlines. His outward actions are "clear"—he changes his clothing several times daily; he breakfasts on roast pigeon; he plays all sorts of games; and he refuses to pray—but their roots remain mysterious.

Some people object to him; they recognize that he oversteps the boundaries. They lack faith in him. Rabbi Ozer, for one, objects but not very strongly (especially because he is swayed by the gold). The effect is overwhelmingly brutal—Frampol is powerless; it yields easily to the gentleman from Cracow. It is possible at this point to object that Singer stacks the cards against the village, does not allow it to have one strong spokesman. But such an objection misses the point—humanity does have little power once it is confronted by gold, wish-fulfilment, false signs, lies.

The ball begins (after a lengthy description of Hodle, a vile, dirty and lascivious girl who lives at the town's edge). Everything is perfect—the food, the costumes, even the weather. Several descriptive words alert us, however, to impending disaster: we are informed that the days are "miraculously" warm and the sun "remarkably large."[11] Miracle, remarkable event— proportions are lost. In a lengthy passage the excessive quality is underlined: "Like rivers of burning sulphur, fiery clouds streamed across the heavens, assuming the shapes of elephants, lions, snakes and monsters. They seemed to be waging a battle in the sky, devouring one another, spitting, breathing fire. It almost seemed to be the River of Fire they watched, where demons tortured the evil-doers amidst glowing coals and heaps of ashes."[12] Fire is constant; it assumes control of the situation; and it ranges everywhere. Not only does the fire remind us of excessive lust, it makes us think of the gold itself. Sexuality, avarice, warfare—the three are linked by the "excessive," obsessive stress upon fire. (Singer is fascinated by fire. This collection, for example, contains a story appropriately entitled "Fire.") But the description also suggests that the real world is one of distortions, weird shapes, asymmetrical patterns. The rational lines waver: "The moon swelled, became vast, blood-red, spotted, scarred, and gave off little light."[13]

The "unnatural" fire dominates the scene. So does the gentleman from Cracow. He urges Frampol to burn brightly, surrendering to lust and avarice. He finally reveals himself as "Chief of the Devils";[14] he displays his tail of live serpents. The citizens' dream of glory have given way to nightmare.

I am impressed by the last section of the story. Singer does not stop with the triumph of Satan—this ending would be easy and melodramatic. Instead he returns to Rabbi Ozer, the surviver of holocaust. (Need I point out this recurring figure in his fiction?) The Rabbi urges Frampol to resist fire and to mourn: "Repent, before it is too late. You have fallen into Satan's snare, but it is my fault, I take the sin upon myself. I am the guilty one. I will be your scapegoat, and you shall remain clean."[15] We do not know his motives (as we did not know the gentleman's), but we respond to his strength. Singer tells us that "the compassion of the Jews is well known."[16] *It is this compassion, born after holocaust, which really triumphs.* Frampol is reborn as a result of other towns contributing money, services, blessings.

There aren't any dazzling flames at the end. Frampol learns not to "rekindle" the lust for gold; it relinquishes fiendish fire for the "eternal light" which burns as a memorial to Rabbi Ozer. His sainted spirit, symbolized by a "white pigeon," survives the gentleman from Cracow."[17]

"The Little Shoemakers" begins within a historical framework. We are told that "the name of Abba Shuster is recorded, on parchment, in the annals of the Frampol Jewish community."[18] He is the founder of the family of "little shoemakers"; he appears in the town some time after Chmielnitzki's pogroms. He builds a house "that remained standing until just the other day."[19] The historical events—the pogroms; the construction of the house; the birth of children—are rapidly but firmly described because Singer wants here to establish a sense of destiny. This story, unlike the previous two, gives us the historical fact—the family and the town are completely burdened by time—and reminds us on a smaller scale, of course, of the open, comprehensive novels.

Abba is not characterized at length; nor are his sons; nor are his grandsons. They seem to be less important than their "art"—the eldest son succeeds his father at the workbench—and it is emphasized so much that it assumes a symbolic value. *Shoemaking becomes a kind of covenant between the family and the community and, finally, to the Lord.* It binds all three harmoniously. (Singer mentions the secret formula which is handed on from father to son; it is almost a sign of their magical power.)

Abba, the current father, is a devout man. He thinks of himself as a patriarch, transmitting his knowledge to his sons: "he would imagine that he was Noah, and that his sons were Shem, Ham, and Japhteth. Or else he would see himself in the image of Abraham, Isaac, or Jacob."[20] He serves humbly. Like Calman Jacoby (before his marriage to Clara) he is at home in the town; he refuses to travel in the wide world. It "seems to him that his little town was the navel of the universe and that his own house stood at the very center."[21] Abba is urged to expand his business, build a new house and submit to change. But he remains firm: "There was nothing to change."[22]

It is Gimpel, the eldest son, who decides to rebel and go to America. Although he resembles Ezriel and Asa Bannet—and the narrator of *In My Father's Court* —in his desire to travel and conquer new worlds, he is not completely drawn. (He is, after all, in a parable; he is here to *make a point.*) But his outlines are clear. He is the representative of the future—he says that

"there's no future for me in Frampol"[23]—and he cannot, naturally, accept the town (or the past) as "navel."

Abba remains. He sees all his sons emigrate to the
new world. He begins to wonder about the fate of the
family. Is it cursed? Is it being punished? His questions quickly turn to affirmation: God's will be done.
He survives world wars, massacres, ruins. He hardly
notices forty years rush past. He continues to work
at his art, singing of survival. (He is, in certain re-
spects, like Singer himself writing in a "dead" language.)

The Nazis come. Abba must abandon the house of
his forefathers and wander in the countryside. But he
continues to regard himself as "his own great-great-
grandfather, who had fled Chmielnitzski's pogroms,
and whose name is recorded in the annals of Frampol."[24] He carries on his name and lesson. Even after
he arrives in America—his sons have sent for him—he
is still devout, unassimilated, and pure.

The last section of the story is entitled "The
American Heritage." It is especially vivid. The sons,
grandchildren, and great-grandchildren give up at
least for one day their assimilated patterns to honor
Abba's arrival. They have a feast. They share, as best
they can, the Frampol legends, the old laws.

But it is only after many months that Abba is
"reborn." He begins to fix shoes; he "saves" himself
by this art. The activity is so inspirational that the sons
join him: "They had not forgotten their heritage, nor
had they lost themselves among the unworthy."[25] They
sing once more of survival.

Thus "The Little Shoemaker," like "Gimpel the
Fool" and "The Gentleman from Cracow," is a story
of belief. It is less ironic, playful, or dark than the
others, but it manages to render the Jewish experience

—of survival in the face of holocaust and emigration to America—in a concise way. It is parable, history, and sociology at the same time.

The Spinoza of Market Street (1961) is another wide-ranging collection of stories.

The title story is clearly one of Singer's best. Dr. Nahum Fischelson is an avid reader of Spinoza—as was the narrator of *In My Father's Court*—and he knows "every proposition, every proof, every corollary, every note by heart."[26] The *Ethics* is his holy text. He attempts to live by its ideas, believing that "according to Spinoza morality and happiness were identical, and that the most moral deed a man could perform was to indulge in some pleasure which was not contrary to reason."[27] Dr. Fischelson is, then, a mature Asa Heschel Bannet or Ezriel; he lives according to a strict moral code (which, of course, has less to do with orthodox Judaism than with rationalism).

But he is a bit obsessive in his life pattern. He has surrendered so completely that he resembles the inhabitants of Goray—he cannot look *ironically* and *playfully* at it. He cannot stop his inflexibility. He gazes at the Milky Way and disregards Market Street below his window. He is between worlds; he is not completely alive on earth. It is, of course, ironic that he condemns the "vainest of passions"[28] exhibited by the masses because he is immersed in his own passion for rationalism. He shuns the unpredictable, fearing that "irrational" events and people will destroy him. He repeats compulsively: "All was determined, all necessary, and a man of reason had no right to worry."[29] The fears remain: "Nevertheless, worry invaded his brain, and buzzed about like the flies."[30]

Singer describes the unpredictable, "mad" things

surrounding Dr. Fischelson (even as the doctor worships his text). In the very first paragraph we read of a "variety of insects"[31] buzzing around the candle flame. These creatures disturb Dr. Fischelson; they are strangely uncontrollable and resemble, without his knowledge, his own confusion over flames. (Fire is again dwelt upon as it was in "The Gentleman from Cracow.") A tomcat howls; he calls it "ignorant savage" and threatens it with a broom handle. He views the people in the street as noisy, buzzing, agitated animals. He dreams of the burning red sky, of bells ringing. These details undercut the calm rationalism of Dr. Fischelson; they demonstrate that he is on the edge (like Yasha on the balcony?).

Black Dobbe, his neighbor, is a coarse, unpredictable, and illiterate spinster. She is an "emissary" from the other world. When she visits him, asking him to read a letter, she finds that he is deathly ill. She proceeds to nurse him back to robust (?) health.

The two are, naturally, frightened of each other. Black Dobbe thinks of "witches, of black mirrors and corpses wandering around at night and terrifying women . . ."[32] when she gazes at him. Dr. Fischelson considers her the arch-representative of Market Street. But their differences also attract them. Gradually they think of marriage.

The marriage is presented as a "miracle." It is appropriate because it is perfectly symbolic (and in keeping with the stylized, dream-like tone). Singer is wonderfully ironic. He does not sentimentalize the miracle; he goes so far as to hint that it is black magic. He leaves the outlines fuzzy.

The last paragraph also leaves the matter open; it fails to give a "final solution" because it fights such a simple pattern (a pattern which resembles Dr. Fischelson's former life-design). Dr. Fischelson continues to stare at the heavens—he has just discovered his sexual potency—and to think about "destined courses in un-bounded space":[33] "Yes, the divine substance was ex-tended and had neither beginning nor end; it was ab-solute, indivisible, eternal, without duration, infinite in its attributes."[34] He sees himself as the product of an "unbroken chain of causes and effects."[35] He is, how-ever, "shaky" and unsure. He murmurs: "Divine Spi-noza, forgive me. I have become a fool."[36] There is great irony here. It is possible to claim that he is still a fool because he does not realize that his marriage is a divine sign, a life-giving miracle. If only he were truly foolish like Gimpel—that is, wise and vital—he would be less shaky. "Fool" means at least two things in the line just quoted—in its ambiguity it defeats the simple-minded "madness" of Dr. Fischelson.

"Shiddah and Kuziba" is only seven pages long, but it creates an extremely powerful impression. The opening sentence introduces the inverted, odd perspec-tive from which the story is told: "Shiddah and her child, Kuziba, a schoolboy, were sitting nine yards in-side the earth at a place where two ledges of rock came together and an underground stream was flow-ing."[37] The juxtaposition of demonic mother and son (no less "schoolboy") and subhuman perspective is wonderfully done, especially when we read that Ku-ziba "looked like his mother"[38] (how natural in having wings of a bat and feet like a chicken).

There is a great deal of enlightening play when Singer explains the schooling of Kuziba. Like any child the creature is afraid of the unknown, the "de-monic"; in this case, however, he is afraid of light and humanity. He is comforted when he hears that they are "safe here—far from light and far from human beings. It's as dark as Egypt here, thank God, and as silent as a cemetery."[39] The playfulness suddenly shifts to rage. It is almost as if Singer cannot refrain from attacking humanity for imperfection. Man is said by Shiddah to have "a white skin but inside he is red. He shouts as if he were strong, but really he is weak and shaky. Throw a stone and he breaks; use a thong and he bleeds."[40] Man is condemned for the inability to consider new perspectives (new worlds possibly inhabited by Shiddah and Kuziba) and to escape from pride. It is no wonder that Kuziba is afraid of humanity; he, like us, yields to the graphic, one-sided sermon.

Part Two continues the juxtapositions of natural (that is to say, human) and supernatural elements. Kuziba cries out in his sleep; he is dreaming about a man (horror of horrors!). He has to be reassured by a lullaby which asks God to save them from Light and Words and Man. While he dozes, he is "cradled" by his mother.

There is a lengthy theological passage. Shiddah remembers her husband (who does not live at home) and his study of silence. She pursues the idea of silence: "He who has reached the final point, the last degree of silence, knows nothing of time and space, of death and lust. There male and female are forever united; will and deed are the same. This last silence is God."[41] I think that by his inversion Singer praises the words of men (including, of course, his own fiction). These words may be fuzzy and imprecise—how can they capture the supernatural?—*but they are all we have; they separate us from bats and devils who worship deep silence*. It is beautifully ironic that Shiddah *expounds at length* about silence. Even devils must attempt to shape thoughts in language!

Shiddah also has dreams. She imagines, as any loving mother would, how her boy will grow up (and become a big devil!); how she will take care of her grandchildren (by delousing their heads!); and how her husband will succeed and be offered "the throne in the Abyss of the Great Female, a thousand miles away from the surface where no one had heard of man and his insanity."[42]

But her dreams are shattered by a terrible thundering. The holocaust has come! (We expect it from Singer.) There is the noise of a machine—man-made, of course—as it grinds the rock which they inhabit; the noise reduces her dream of silence to dust. She prays to Satan, to Lilith, and "to all the other powers which maintain creation."[43] But her prayer is not answered. Ironically she moves *upward*, to earth, where she will establish a new home, build a new "manor."

The last paragraph is especially chilling (as the playful irony I have mentioned is dropped). Shiddah knows that "the last victory would be to darkness."[44] Then "the remembrance of man and his abominations would be nothing but a bad dream which God had spun out for a while to distract Himself in His eternal night."[45]

Thus "Shiddah and Kuziba," unlike the other stories I have discussed (or, for that matter, most of the novels), ends on a hopeless note—at least for mankind. Although it is possible to claim that Shiddah is an absolutist who cannot see clearly (and dreams of salvation through miracle), it is still difficult to escape the fact that Singer apparently agrees with her denunciations. He is not joking at the end; he is "fiendish" here.

"The Black Wedding" begins with a description of "apathetic" Rabbi Aaron Naphtali. He allows the study house to decay—we are told that "toadstools grew unmolested on the walls"—and he spends his time "practicing miracle—working cabala."[46] He is, obviously, a false spiritual leader (who resembles in part the various ineffectual fathers Singer has portrayed).

Rabbi Aaron Naphtali is so involved with "signs" that he allows the black hosts to destroy him. He hears steps on the roof; he notes candles extinguished suddenly. Is he really able to see vengeful devils? Or does he merely project his madness upon the world? These questions are raised but not answered by Singer (as is true in most of his "demonic" fictions). We are offered facts to support both kinds of explanation; we are free to interpret as we wish. Thus Singer allows our freedom, compelling us to use it and to behave *openly* (unlike Rabbi Aaron).

The madness extends to the Rabbi's daughter, Hindele. She reads esoteric books; she goes into seclusion as does her father. After he dies, she is urged to marry Reb Simon. She cannot stop crying: "She cried at the celebration of the writing of the marriage contract, she cried when the tailors fitted her trousseau, she cried when she was led to the ritual bath."[47] We confront the same ambiguous motivations with Hindele. We do not know how to read her. Perhaps it is best to say that like Dr. Fischelson and the Frampol citizens in "The Gentleman from Cracow," she is an obsessive believer; she wants to fit reality into her design (which was mysteriously passed on to her by the Rabbi). She creates "miracles"; she shapes visions.

When Hindele stares at her future husband she apparently realizes "what she had suspected long before—that her bridegroom was a demon and that the wedding was nothing but black magic, a satanic hoax."[48] She believes, furthermore, that the wedding is destined to be a Black Wedding. She is alone; she cannot communicate her crazy visions to anyone else. She cannot even tell *us* because we cannot get behind her insights. We see powerfully what she sees; we do not know more than she. We notice, for example, the canopy as "a braid of reptiles," the "hoof" of Reb Simon, a dancing witch, and the "webbed roosters' feet" of the musicians.[49] But we are not sure *why* we (and she) observe these things. In a way we are as unknowledgeable and isolated as Hindele. Singer makes us share in her experience, but he does not completely convince us. He plays a trick.

The story falters after a while because Hindele goes so far in her madness that we cannot assent to it. When she rebels against the child in her womb, calling it "half-frog, half-ape,"[50] she oversteps the boundary. She becomes simply another lunatic; she no longer teases us with her great ambiguity.

The story ends ironically. There is a frame effect which demonstrates that the community (like us) can never understand her tortured delusions: "In Tzivkev and in the neighborhood the tidings spread that Hindele had given birth to a male child by Reb Simon of Yampol. The mother had died in childbirth."[51] The previous madness has dissolved; calm objectivity conquers all. I prefer the ending (which is open and playful) to the somewhat easy condition of Hindele before her death.

"The Man Who Came Back" is more playful than "The Black Wedding"; it does not settle for simple madness. It opens brilliantly: "You may not believe it but there are people in the world who were called back."[52] I like the conversational tone—it makes the "miracle" seem natural—which immediately creates a bond between us and the narrator. (The effect is, of

course, completely different from the distancing of
"The Gentleman from Cracow"; it is more like that
of "Gimpel the Fool.") We delight in his descriptions
of Alter, "the man who came back"—the man gives the
narrator "a cookie together with a pinch on the
cheek"[53]—and we are prepared to believe the miracle
when it occurs.

There is no loud noise; the miracle is as plain and
folksy as the previous descriptions. On his deathbed
Alter responds to his wife's urging and comes back to
this world: "They were just making a move to pull her
away when suddenly the corpse stirred and let out a
deep sigh. She had called him back."[54] Soon he begins
to "wisecrack" once more. He is the same man! (I like
Alter as a jokester; it is appropriate for the entire tone
of the story.)

The narrator says: "Well, things took a turn."[55] It
seems that Alter has changed after all—he looks for
quarrels; he tells his wife to "dress up"; he trims his
beard. He becomes now another Singer "isolato" who
lives apart from the community—always a sin!—because of his inflexible vision. (He makes us think of
Hawthorne's heroes.)

Alter begins to court the newly-arrived barber's
sister-in-law; he admires her depravity (so unlike his
wife's temperament). He falls into lustful pursuit—sex
is characteristically attractive and repulsive here as in
other Singer fictions—and he is only "saved" by the
woman's quick departure. But Alter wants freedom;
he asks for a divorce and gets it. He is on his own.

He becomes, for the second time, a new person.
(There is almost a parody of resurrection.) He considers himself a real thief—a leader of "roughnecks."
Ironically he dies as he asserts his power. The story
ends with a vivid, detailed scene. Alter's corpse "be-

haves" strangely: "Pieces were dropping from his body. The face could not be recognized, it was a shapeless pulp. It was said that when he was being cleansed for burial, an arm came off, and then a foot. . . ."[56] The physical decay symbolizes convincingly his spiritual decline.

There is a sermon by the narrator but it is brief and ambiguous: "it is not proper to recall the dying."[57] I take it that he means we should accept our limitations with humility—we should not, like Alter and his wife, try to work miracles. Something, however, is left unsaid. How did the "deluded" woman bring him back? What exactly are the limits of our souls? These questions are complicated by the narrator's own question: "And who knows how many men who were called back are out in the world today?"[58] We are left finally, as in the other stories, with a sense of unwilling suspension.

Short Friday (1964) contains at least three stories which are worthy of extended analysis.

"Blood" begins with a prophetic, arresting sentence: "The cabalists know that the passion for blood and the passion for flesh have the same origin, and this is the reason 'Thou shalt not kill' is followed by 'Thou shalt not commit adultery.' "[59] It alerts us, first of all, to the word "passion" which, for Singer, covers a multitude of sins (or obsessions). For him anything can be a passion—even the desire to avoid passion as in the case of Dr. Fischelson—and he delights in presenting stylized, "one-sided" characters who are consumed by compulsive pursuit of their lusts. The sentence also indicates the linkage of lust and violence, a linkage which has been apparent in *Satan in Goray*, *The Ma-*

gician of Lublin and, for that matter, most of the fictions I have discussed.

"Blood" is especially powerful because the passions are clarified by striking images. Risha, the "man-killer," likes red meat; even though she is married to Reb Falik, she is attracted to the ritual slaughterer, Reuben. She seems to love his job—"bloody" as it is—more than him. When she first notices him, for example, he swings a slaughtered chicken "as if about to toss it"[60] into a woman's face: "Meanwhile the chicken, its throat slit, fell to the ground where it fluttered about, flapping its wings in its attempt to fly and spattering Reuben's boots with blood. Finally the little rooster gave a last start and then lay still, one glassy eye and its slit neck facing up to God's heaven."[61] I have quoted the passage because it suggests the roots of the relationship of Risha and Reuben. Both are killers, trying to slaughter others (finally themselves) for their own nourishment. They violently defile the world. (It is interesting in this context to mention that Singer is a vegetarian.) They disregard Heaven.

Their courtship is presented as a hunt. Reuben shows his strength (and capacity for passion) by drawing the "bluish edge of the blade across the nail of his index finger."[62] He stares at her as he slaughters a gander. Later he kills a rooster and this so excites them that they soon sleep together: "In their amorous play, she asked him to slaughter her. Taking her head, he bent it back and fiddled with his finger across her throat."[63] Lovingly they call each other "murderers."

We respond to these violent passages and tend to think of Risha and Reuben as animals (stronger than the ones they slit). This effect is precisely what Singer wants. He does not give us full-bodied people; he creates "caricatures" (or grotesques) who have renounced their ability to function spiritually. They are vivid (livid?), dream-like, and half-alive.

Risha becomes the more powerful. First she opens a butcher shop (hiring Reuben as a slaughterer); then she decides, against all laws, to become a slaughterer without studying the orthodox laws and, eventually, to sell non-kosher meat. The more she commands, the less Reuben obeys. Risha oversteps all the boundaries —she becomes "masculine," corrupt, mad, and pagan— despite his growing resistance. She thinks of him, finally, as "only a hero against a weak chicken and a tethered ox."[64] She sends him away.

Her victory is apparently complete when she "kills" her husband. Reb Falik, unlike Reuben, is half-blind and so deaf that he cannot cope with reality. His religious studies do not help him. When he sees Risha enter with a knife in her hand, he collapses.

Risha converts. She sings in Polish. She grows fat. She becomes an animal (more so than before): she "utters sounds that resembled the cackling of fowl, the grunting of pigs, the death rattles of oxen."[65] She even dreams of slaughtered creatures—gradually she has become the victim!—and her dreams reinforce the fantastic and hallucinatory story: "bulls gored her with their horns, pigs shoved their snouts into her face and bit her; roosters cut her flesh to ribbons with their spurs."[66]

The story concludes with a characteristic frame effect. We are told that the town is terrified by a "carnivorous animal"[67]—it is said to be a bear, a wolf, or a demon. The butchers decide to chase and kill it. They do—it howls and falls to the ground. They then discover the animal is Risha, now a werewolf. They are victorious.

The final victory, however, remains for their children and grandchildren who dance near Risha's grave (outside of town): *"Thou shalt not suffer a witch to live. . . ."*[68] They celebrate ritualistically; they declare an end to "bloodshed." I am again unconvinced—as I think Singer himself is—by such contrived victory, but I am impressed by the unforgettable passion of the slaughterer.

"The Last Demon" begins with another startling first sentence: "I, a demon, bear witness that there are no more demons left."[69] The contradiction—how can a demon denounce *other* demons?—and the directness contribute to our amazement. We wonder how Singer can follow the introduction.

He is able to surpass it by means of his playful irony. The narrator tells us that he is a Jew—that he is *chosen:* "I don't have to tell you that I am a Jew. What else, a Gentile? I've heard that there are Gentile demons, but I don't know any, nor do I wish to know him."[70] He is, indeed, a scholar of sorts, gaining sustenance from a Yiddish storybook and claiming that "Hebrew letters have a weight of their own."[71] He sees things in a long-range perspective (as did Shiddah) and he wonders why he is destined to spend his days—actually "days" is an inappropriate word because he is eternal—in such a wasteland as Tishevitz, a "God-forsaken village."[72]

He tells us about his past in the town, speaking in a rambling, folksy, and idiomatic manner (as did Gimpel). He uses the present tense: "as for me time stands still."[73] He looks for mischief; he wants to earn a name for himself. (He hates being just another slave to his boss.) He finds two kinds of obstacles—would-be sinners and holy men.

His comments about the sinners are pithy. He

realizes, using the words of a mentor, that there are "petty men, petty sins. Today someone covets another man's broom, tomorrow he fasts and puts peas in his shoes."[74] Sins are no longer meaningful—they are mere whims. They have lost value; so have the demons who thrive only when human beings *care*. Then, of course, there are the other sinners who go to such extremes that they are willing to try *anything*. They also give little struggle or sense of mission accomplished to demons.

So the narrator decides to try his luck with the Rabbi of Tishevitz. He will make his mark by converting a holy man into a sinner. This is his mission, his life—goal. He offers him the usual temptations—money, women, and fame—but they are not particularly appealing. He finds himself in a dirty mood. He rages; he wants to run away. He starts behaving like a child.

The narrator decides to concentrate upon the snare of pride. It "has the strongest meshes."[75] (He is probably right if we take into account the self-love of such typical Singer characters as Dr. Fischelson, Alter, Yasha *et al.*) He praises the Rabbi, calling him "saint" and "wise man." He insists that Tishevitz is no place for him. (It is ironic that he projects his own feelings upon the rabbi.) But he again fails when the Rabbi asks to study his feet (looking for claws).

Singer does not stop here as would most writers. He maintains that one victory over the devils is not enough to save the world. The narrator takes us to the immediate "present." He shows the holocaust: "The rabbi was martyred on a Friday in the month of Nisan. The community was slaughtered, the holy books burned, the cemetery desecrated."[76] There is now no need for demons; the narrator is "the last, a refugee."[77]

Singer presents one final turn. The narrator sustains himself by reading a Yiddish storybook. He is fascinated not by the religious messages but by the Hebrew letters. Surely this nourishment is symbolic! I assume that like his demon, Singer believes that only the word—even in "fictions"—can sustain us by helping us to understand the snares of existence.

"Short Friday," unlike "Blood" and "The Last Demon," is a story of fulfillment. (It resembles *The Slave*.) Although I do not think that it is as successful as the darker ones, I am still fond of it.

The first sentence is important: "In the village of Lapschitz lived a tailor named Schmul-Leibele with his wife, Shoshe."[78] It alerts us to their marriage which *defines* them. *They exist only in terms of this relationship.* We read in the next few lines that Schmul-Leibele is an incompetent tailor—he "had once sewn a pair of trousers with the fly off to one side"[79]—and he functions socially because of his competent wife.

Schmul-Leibele is not handsome or graceful. His hands and feet are too large for his body; his forehead "bulged on either side as is common in simpletons";[80] he walks with heavy steps. The physical details are emphasized to stress his unattractive external appearance and, consequently, to make us ask *what* Shoshe sees in him. The answer is simple. It is his piety.

Schmul-Leibele is well-versed in all the laws. He never misses a sermon. He recites the Psalms each day. He reminds us of Gimpel because of his divine "foolishness"—his ability to believe in the goodheartedness of men (who taunt him).

The couple relish the Sabbaths in winter. Shoshe

busies herself with the preparation of the meal: She
bustles "about efficiently with spatulas, pokers, ladles
and goosewing dusters. . . ."[81] He bathes. He walks
to the synagogue. Singer spends so much time on their
ritualistic behavior that the couple become less important than the roles they play—they *serve* the Sabbath;
they don't, like a Risha, force their religion to submit to
them. Unfortunately, they are not interesting human
beings, and their spiritual activities do not compen-
sate for their fictional simplicity.

Singer turns to one Friday, the "shortest Friday
of the year."[82] Their activities are, of course, the same.
They glory in being near each other. They eat a full
meal. They sing hymns. They go to bed.

It is at this point that the story takes on a different
life—a life of playful irony characteristic of the best
Singer. Schmul-Liebele cannot resist making love to
Shoshe. His piety surrenders to lust. They sleep at
last. But their sleep is their undoing. They die of gas
inhalation. Even in death—what togetherness!—they
share one dream. (Again Singer employs a dream to
suggest the "unreality" of existence.) They dream of
Schmul-Liebele's death: "The Burial-Society brethren
came by, picked him up, lit candles by his head, opened
the windows, intoned the prayer to justify God's or-
dainment. After they washed him on the ablution
board, carried him on a stretcher to the cemetery."[83]
Now they believe that they are still alive, but their
"short Friday" has turned into an eternal holy day.
They are out of time; they are out of their own
sleeping bodies.

The questions—how exactly did they die? did they
die because of *lust?*—are not resolved when we are
informed that "the brief years of turmoil and temptation had come to an end. Schmul-Liebele and Shoshe

had reached the true world. Man and wife grew silent."[84] Singer uses the final word "Paradise," but he has not convinced us that the couple have earned it. He allows them to know where they have gone; he keeps us in the dark (or dazzling light).

"Short Friday" is, then, an odd story because it evades answering basic questions of motivation; it settles for grace or Paradise. It is a half-wish-fulfillment.

The title story of Singer's next collection, *The Séance* (1968), is set in New York, but it draws upon the themes, characters, and symbols of his more exotic *stetl* (small village) stories. It is also a story of belief.

The first paragraph demonstrates that Lotte Kopitzky is a believer in the other world; she does things "in a state of trance and at the direction of her control —Bhaghavar Krishna, a Hindu sage supposed to have lived in the fourth century."[85] Her paintings are "automatic" and grotesque. Her apartment is also strange: a red bulb illuminates the room; the windows are covered with heavy drapes. These details are carefully chosen to suggest the claustrophobic, shadowy recesses of her psyche.

Dr. Zorach Kalisher observes her. He considers himself a "fool"—one of Singer's favorite words—because he sits waiting for the Hindu sage. He is half-skeptic, half anti-rationalist—he hopes for some sign. His failure as lover, writer, and spiritual guide is symbolized not only by his miracle seeking but by his sexual impotence. He is "married" to crazy Mrs. Kopitzky; they feed on each other like Risha and Reuben (although less brutally).

Singer elaborates upon the séances. He demonstrates how they are self-serving, mad rituals. (They parody orthodox rituals.) The Hindu sage never really

commits himself to Mrs. Kopitzky; she merely mut-
ters his hazy words about the "Masters," the "Heavenly Hierarchy," the "Powers of Light."[86] She offers
news of Nella, the girl Dr. Kalisher left behind in Europe many years ago. Recently "Nella" has appeared
as an apparition in the dark corridor. The séances are
obviously *masquerades*—Dr. Kalisher knows that Mrs.
Kopitzky has hired the ghost, but he nevertheless goes
along with the game out of curiosity and longing; Mrs.
Kopitzky hopes to bind herself more tightly to him—
but they satisfy the secret desires they both have to
believe, if only momentarily, in mystery. They "play"
to get out of their tormented selves; they don't realize
that such play is as grotesque as its source. (I should
add that the aspects of play call to mind Singer's delight in play-within-play, dream-within-dream. He
likes, as in "The Man Who Came Back," to have a
kind of double effect. Indeed one of the stories in
Gimpel the Fool is entitled "The Mirror.")

Dr. Kalisher cannot completely escape from himself. He is locked in his body's cage—as the windows
are covered by the drapes?—and he realizes his mortality. He is aware of his prostate condition. During the
ritual this evening, he gets a "sign" from the sage, but
he disregards it for another: he has to urinate. When
he goes to the bathroom, he sees the actress who plays
Nella, the apparition. He is hypnotized; he "wets himself like a child."[87]

The next section begins with Dr. Kalisher's comment: "Well, I've reached the bottom."[88] It is an interesting one because it suggests, ironically, that he
recognizes his condition. *He has seen the truth.* (He
is, of course, a "visionary" throughout the story.) He
decides to go home, but he has lost "all sense of direction in that labyrinth of an apartment."[89] He is again

like a lost, wet child. He allows Mrs. Kopitzky to mother him: he sits "stiff, wet, childishly guilty and helpless, and yet with that inner quiet that comes from illness."[90] He puts on her late husband's clothing—the detail is symbolic—and loses whatever identity he now possesses.

The retreat into childhood; the loss of identity; the shock of recognition—all are conveyed beautifully by Singer's meticulous details. We are told, for example, that Dr. Kalisher "stood with his upper part fully dressed and his pants off like some mad jester."[91] He steps into "a pair of loose drawers that were as cool as shrouds."[92] (He is "dead," no longer the adult Dr. Kalisher.) He sees himself as a child in Europe dressing up in a masquerade (of his father no less!) and he sticks out his tongue at his mirror reflection. Finally he blots out everything by sleeping.

The story ends with as much ambiguity as any I have discussed. Dr. Kalisher half-dreams that he must become a new person. He will resurrect himself—the Messiah symbol is vaguely present here (as we would expect from Singer)—by admitting to Mrs. Kopitzky their narcissistic lies, their fakery. When he opens his eyes, however, he asks her: "Has Nella left?"[93] Why does he? Does he realize, "half-asleep" and "amazed at his own words,"[94] that he must love *something* (even if it is unreal)? Can he mean the *real* Nella of his past? The questions are not answered. Instead Singer writes: "Mrs. Kopitzky winced. . . . Her dark eyes were filled with motherly reproach."[95] She has the last words; she will answer his ambiguous question. But she says: "You're laughing, huh! There is no death, there isn't any. We live forever, and we lose forever. This is the pure truth."[96] The pure truth! Is it that she still lies in her comment (for her own purpose of keeping him)? Is it that she recognizes, as does Singer, the impossibility of escaping from past commitments? The greatness of the story lies ultimately in this play of truth, this ritual of ambiguity, even when answers are desired.

Yoineh Meir, the hero of "The Slaughterer," is a misfit. Although he should have been the Kolomir rabbi—his father and grandfather occupied the position—he is made the town's ritual slaughterer because of "political" opposition. He is completely unhappy with his new role—he is far from being a Risha or Reuben!—and he protests that he cannot bear the sight of blood.

Yoineh Meir tries, nevertheless, to adjust. He even relinquishes his hatred of blood for a short time. He imposes new rigors upon himself. But he can find no ultimate consolation; he refuses to accept the idea of murder (even for religious ends): "The killing of every beast, great or small, caused him as much pain as though he were cutting his own throat. Of all the punishments that could have been visited upon him, slaughtering was the worst."[97]

How can we explain his fears? Do they arise out of childhood traumas? The questions take us to the heart of the matter. Singer does not settle for easy psychoanalysis. He accepts the "obsession" as a religious axiom. He begins with it because it radically questions the facts of life. Thus Yoineh Meir rages with questions. Why should beasts suffer (if they do not have free choice)? Why is some slaughtering good? At what point should bloodshed stop?

The problem is that he cannot resolve his doubts and also escape from his community duties. He is a dangling man. He cannot move in any direction without hurting himself. What irony! The more he chooses life against death (that is, not slaughtering), the more wounded he becomes. He kills himself each day: "He felt as though he were immersed in blood and lymph. His ears were beset by the squawking of hens, the crowing of roosters, the gobbling of geese, the lowing of oxen, the mooing and bleating of calves and goats. . . ."[98] He begins, indeed, to see himself as a slaughtered creature (which he no doubt is).

Yoineh Meir longs to ascend to a different world of light. He wants to fly (as did Yasha). He stares at the sky: "The moon spread a radiance around it. The stars flashed and twinkled, each with its own heavenly secret."[99] He begins to seek death—he feared it previously—as a way to escape.

But the bloody details persist. (Singer "obsessively" presents them): "Under every skin he saw blood. Every neck reminded Yoineh Meir of the knife. Human beings, like beasts, had loins, veins, guts, buttocks."[100] He hates his body and its covering. It is a cage; symbolically, he cannot breathe as the first section ends.

The next section opens calmly (a relief from the growing intensity of bloody details). We are told that the month of Elul brings a "sense of exalted serenity."[101] (The height metaphor is stressed again.) It offers "saffron" yellow leaves, cool breezes, and pale-blue skies. But Elul is, ironically, an especially busy time for slaughterers—"a great many beasts are slaughtered for the New Year";[102] and it makes Yoineh Meir even more distraught than before. He no longer differentiates between beasts and men. Consequently, he dreams of cows with human shape (wearing beards no less!) and he hears voices coming from a slaughtered goat. His dreams are married to his waking visions. He gets up and still listens to frogs with human voices.

Surely he is "mad"—as are most of Singer's characters—but it is difficult to condemn him. His madness creates "an unfamiliar love" for "all that crawls
and flies, breeds and swarms."[103] He believes as an absolutist that "when you slaughter a creature, you
slaughter God. . . ."[104] He cannot reconcile this love
for all creatures and the Lord with the command
(mentioned in the Bible) that He wants ritual slaughter. He finally blasphemes—destroying the holy instru-
ments—and claims that God is a slaughterer!

Yoineh Meir flees to another world; he wants to
cleanse himself after having lived in the world slaugh-
terhouse. He plunges into the river. It is now a river
of blood for him (stained with red droppings from
the sun). His final words are " 'Devouring beast!' "[105]

The end of the story is wonderfully ironic. Yoineh Meir's corpse is cleansed; he is eulogized by the
rabbi and accepted once more by the community. He
is, oddly, "consumed" and used for social nourishment.
In the last line we read that the community (which
has defeated the mad hero) hastily sends for a new
slaughterer. *So the killing continues—for religious purposes.*

"Cockadoodledoo," unlike the other stories, is a
fable. The narrator is a "great-grandson of the rooster
who perched on King Solomon's chair";[106] he knows
languages and speaks directly to us. He claims that we
do not know how to use words properly—we use a
"lot" for our purposes!—and that, in effect, we often
babble. The tables are turned (as in "Shiddah and Kuziba"); the inversion—how dare a rooster tell us how
to speak and think!—startles us with an unfamiliar
perspective.

The rooster is a "believer," like his human coun-
terparts in most Singer stories, and he affirms his belief

in the very first word he utters: "cockadoodledoo." The word covers many different tones, life experiences, accents, and styles; but it is above all, an affirmative sign embracing the order of the universe. This is not to imply that "cockadoodledoo" blots out knowledge of pain and suffering. The rooster tells us that he knows "the end all too well: death. Whether they'll make a sacrifice of me for Yom Kippur, Whether they'll put me aside until Passover, Succoth or for the Sabbath of Moses' Song of the Red Sea, the slaughterer waits, the knife is sharp. . . ."[107] He is philosophical about his eventful end, believing as he does that he is part of a long line of suffering creatures. He possesses great humility. (He resembles a Calman Jacoby or Yasha the Penitent.) He will survive in spite of itching beak, burning comb, and trembling tongue.

The rooster feels in his bones that there exists a "heavenly rooster—his image is our own; and there is a heavenly Cockadoodledoo."[108] He prays to this higher being, using the magical word for sustenance. Ironically, he cannot reveal the meaning of "cockadoodledoo" to us; human beings cannot believe purely, humbly, and wholeheartedly.

Now that the rooster has stated the tenets of his faith (even though he knows that he cannot convert us), he has the time to ramble. He spins anecdotes; he gossips. First he tells us about hens—their hypocrisy, their attractiveness, and their cluck-clucking. He has five wives, and he describes them in terms that could fit all women. They are, for example, easy-going, jealous, or wise. But the playfulness exists in the sudden turns of phrase. Tsip is oversexed and she lays tiny eggs "with bloody specks."[109] Chips loves the rooster with a "chaste love"; she is said to cluck "with a soft-tongued cluck."[110] Because we are never certain about the human and non-human characteristics of the hens (or of the narrator himself), we laugh uneasily. We do more: we begin to realize that *all* creatures are vital.

The rooster relates tales of his hens, but he is more interested in religious traditions. He returns to the matter of faith—as do all of Singer's characters. He tells us of a miracle. One day he waited for the slaughter; he wept and prayed. The end was near. (Even Singer's roosters sense the holocaust!): "It seemed as if the world had asked the ultimate question and was waiting for an answer: yes or no, one way or another."[111]

Suddenly he heard a "new voice, a new word."[112] He was reborn: "I stuck my beak in my feathers and pinched my own skin to see if it hurt. Suddenly: cockadoodledoo!"[113] The sound thrilled him so much that he continues to this day to preach—that is why he speaks to us!—and to reveal the secrets of true faith.

He spreads the word: "Happy is he who believes. A time will come when all will see and hear, and the cockadoodledoo of the Rooster on High will ring throughout heaven and earth."[114] He shouts triumphantly (in the last word of the story): "Cockadoodledoo!"

Surely the secret of the rooster (as he admits) is beyond us. Unfortunately, we want to know *how* to see truth; we cannot easily give ourselves to the magical word. Thus we admire "Cockadoodledoo" while we identify more with suffering Yoineh Meir or Dr. Kalisher. There is no doubt, however, that the three stories which vary in setting, technique, and symbol—but not in the theme of faith—are among Singer's greatest fictions.

A Friend of Kafka (1970), Singer's latest collection, does not contain any story as good as the three I have just explicated. Although the twenty-one stories in this collection are set in strikingly different places—we move from New York to Warsaw to Tel Aviv—they are similar because of one recurring theme: the world itself is miraculous, illogical, and exotic. One of Singer's characters groans: "If a miracle does happen, it is explained as natural. In my time we could find miracles everywhere."[115] These stories strive to capture the miracle in the commonplace (or vice versa), and demonstrate thereby that cosmic mysteries still exist.

Singer is so concerned with the miracle that at times he thrusts it at us. It is unearned and gratuitous. I am thinking of such stories as "The Key." Bessie Popkin, an old woman, lives alone in New York, and loses the key to her apartment. She sees the world as strange and hostile; she suffers from demons, imps, Evil Powers. We are not really told why she acts this way. Age? Madness? Senility? Such causes are possible. The important thing is that Singer wants to join Bessie as outcast and to recognize, at least partially, the chaos of city life. He is effective here (if we forget about causes and motives). But when his old heroine gets a substitute key to her apartment—we are to take the key as metaphysical as well—and learns to respect "others," we are somewhat disappointed. We rebel against such easy miracles, such false wisdom.

Singer is at his best when he refuses to give us any "final solutions." "The Cafeteria" is also set in New York; it presents a world coming apart. The narrator introduces the subject when he asks: "Whose turn is next?"[116] Who will become crazy? Who will die?

(Many of the stories deal with illness and old age.) He is a more interesting character than Bessie because he is able to distinguish between appearance and reality. (Or so he thinks at first.) He is, indeed, the keen observer of his friends and his own feelings.

When he loses the ability to understand what is happening, we are powerfully troubled. He cannot grasp the motives of a younger woman, Esther, who suddenly appears in the cafeteria. They come closer, but her experience in Europe during World War II obsesses her. There is no real communion (as there was at the end of "The Key").

Esther drifts away and when they meet again, she startles the narrator with her vision. She has seen Hitler in the cafeteria! "I went in and saw a scene I will not forget to the last day of my life. The tables were shoved together and around them sat men in white robes, like doctors or orderlies, all with swastikas on their sleeves. At the head sat Hitler, I beg you to hear me out—even a deranged person sometimes deserves to be listened to."[117] The vision is so bizarre (or "miraculous") that we, like the narrator, are tempted to reject it as mere insanity.

But Singer does not stop here. The rational narrator continues to explicate the vision. He begins with insanity—"This metropolis has all the symptoms of a mind gone berserk"—but ends with faith: "I thought about what Esther had told me of seeing Hitler in the cafeteria. . . . If time and space are nothing more than forms of perception, as Kant argues, and quality, quantity, causality are only categories of thinking, why shouldn't Hitler confer with his Nazis in a cafeteria on Broadway?"[118] The mysteries remain and deepen (especially when Esther is seen after her death). There is no useful "key."

"Forms of perception." The phrase is perhaps the clue to Singer's tense ambiguities in his best stories. He does not allow us to rest with closed facts (and worlds). He suggests, by using obsessive heroes, that there are at least two reasons for the vision of miracles: (1) the hero wants to perceive the miracle and hallucinates, (2) the hero sees what is actually there—the miracle itself. I have suggested that in "The Cafeteria" we are left with both possibilities (unlike "The Key"). It is up to us to find the "key," the proper "form of perception."

Singer is thus a valuable spiritual guide. He compels us to discover if, to use a title from one of the finest stories in the collection, "Something Is There." Perhaps we are forced like the rabbi of Bechev in that story to waver between heresy and belief—he claims that there are no heretics; even heresy is a kind of belief—before we accept the presence of supernatural light. The matter is much more complicated. Singer insists in the same story that we cannot share our "forms of perception" with anyone else—rabbi, author, or coreligionist. We are, after all, alone. We must make our own "keys."

Singer's message is ultimately beyond hope or despair. It is almost ghost-like (to use one of his favorite words): *dimly recognize the miracle.* Yes! But how? And when?

5

Conclusion

I have tried to introduce the reader to Singer's world. It is a difficult task to accomplish in such small space. I hope, however, that I have demonstrated recurring themes, characters, and symbols.

Singer is a religious writer. He is interested primarily in the nature of faith, especially when it is tested by holocaust or crisis. How far should one accept the family, the community and the universe? What is the limit of rebellion? Should Jews be "modern" (that is, create new laws) or old-fashioned? Such difficult questions appear not only in the comprehensive, open novels but in the closed novels and short stories as well. There is, after all, a unified—shall we call it obsessive?—vision behind *The Family Moskat* and "Cockadoodledoo."

I have suggested that at times Singer is so eager to devote his energy to questions of faith that he turns to stereotyped characters—the rebellious Yasha or Ezriel; the devout Calman or Schmul-Leibele—and that we feel they are rather easily understood. They are then lifeless and programmatic. There is no doubt that Singer is more comfortable with tense, ambivalent heroes than with humble ones. I am especially impressed, to name only a few, by Yoineh Meir of "The Slaughterer," the narrator of *In My Father's Court*, and Dr. Kalisher of *The Séance*.

I think—tentatively, tentatively!—Singer will be remembered more for his short stories and closed novels than for his open novels. He is at home in confined space; he can pursue obsessively symbolic details so that these become intense, dramatic, and "divine." The blood in "Blood" and "The Slaughterer," for example, becomes an overwhelming "character" or force; it is so powerful that it enslaves the different heroes. The entire effect is consquently a dream-like atmos-

phere—hallucinatory, savage, and "mad"—which flourishes best in Singer's short stories and links them to the
stories of Kafka, Poe, or Gogol.

Singer is not an innovator. He uses traditional
forms—fable, folktale, and sermon—because he regards
himself as a storyteller. When he is writing well—that
is, most of the time!—he is able to relate the most extraordinary, unbelievable events in a matter-of-fact
tone. He never loses grip of the tension between the
daily occurrence and the "miracle." Indeed he sees the
miracle in the newspaper, the divine in the material experience. He remains remarkably *open*.

I do not want to belabor my conclusion. I assume
that he will be read for a long time, and that his fictions will remain fresh and mysterious even after they
are briefly introduced by future critics.

Notes

1. *The Memoirs*

1. *In My Father's Court* (New York: Farrar, Straus and Giroux, 1966), p. vii.
2. *Ibid.*, p. 11.
3. *Ibid.*
4. *Ibid.*
5. *Ibid.*, p. 15.
6. *Ibid.*, p. 27.
7. *Ibid.*, p. 79.
8. *Ibid.*, p. 178.
9. *Ibid.*
10. *Ibid.*, p. 182.
11. *Ibid.*, p. 239.
12. *Ibid.*
13. *Ibid.*, p. 240.
14. *Ibid.*, p. 243.
15. *Ibid.*, p. 247.
16. *Ibid.*
17. *Ibid.*, p. 256.
18. *Ibid.*
19. *Ibid.*, p. 261.
20. *Ibid.*, p. 265.

21. *Ibid.*, p. 275.
22. *Ibid.*, pp. 300-301.
23. *Ibid.*, p. 302.
24. *Ibid.*, p. 305.

2. *The Open Novels*

1. Ben Siegel, *Isaac Bashevis Singer* (Minneapolis: University of Minnesota Press, 1969), p. 12.
2. *The Family Moskat* (New York: Farrar, Straus, and Giroux, 1966), p. 13.
3. *Ibid.*, p. 46.
4. *Ibid.*, p. 65. Chanukah (or Hanukah) is the Jewish Feast of Lights or Feast of Dedication. It is a celebration of the victory of the Maccabees in 165 B.C. over the Syrians; after cleaning the Temple of Syrian idols, the Jews found a miraculous cruse of oil with which they were able to light their holy lamps for eight days.
5. The Hasidic movement emphasized joy and love rather than formal learning. It was founded in the 1700s in Poland and spread to other Jewish communities in Eastern Europe.
6. *The Family Moskat*, p. 81.
7. *Ibid.*
8. *Ibid.*, p. 140.
9. *Ibid.*, p. 201.
10. *Ibid.*, p. 238.
11. *Ibid.*, p. 287.
12. *Ibid.*, p. 369.
13. *Ibid.*, p. 382.
14. *Ibid.*, p. 398.
15. *Ibid.*
16. *Ibid.*, p. 574. Passover is the Jewish festival of freedom. It celebrates the exodus from Egypt. The Passover feast celebrated at home is called *seder*.

17. *Ibid.*, p. 578.
18. *Ibid.*, p. 596.
19. *Ibid.*, p. 611.
20. *Ibid.*
21. *The Manor* (New York: Farrar, Straus, and Giroux, 1967), author's note.
22. *Ibid.*, p. 4.
23. *Ibid.*, p. 6.
24. *Ibid.*, p. 23.
25. *Ibid.*, p. 24.
26. *Ibid.*, p. 123.
27. *Ibid.*, p. 127.
28. *Ibid.*, p. 133.
29. *Ibid.*, p. 136.
30. *Ibid.*, p. 187.
31. *Ibid.*, p. 202.
32. *Ibid.*, p. 242.
33. *Ibid.*, p. 308.
34. *Ibid.*, p. 343.
35. *Ibid.*, p. 351.
36. *Ibid.*, p. 387.
37. *Ibid.*, p. 394.
38. *Ibid.*, p. 435.
39. *Ibid.*, p. 442.
40. *The Estate* (New York: Farrar, Straus and Giroux, 1969), p. 3.
41. *Ibid.*, p. 44.
42. *Ibid.*
43. *Ibid.*, p. 60.
44. *Ibid.*, p. 61.
45. *Ibid.*, p. 81.
46. *Ibid.*, p. 83.
47. *Ibid.*, p. 94.
48. *Ibid.*, p. 169.
49. *Ibid.*, p. 163.
50. *Ibid.*, p. 180.
51. *Ibid.*, pp. 197-198.
52. *Ibid.*, p. 246.

53. *Ibid.*, p. 365.
54. *Ibid.*, p. 288.
55. *Ibid.*
56. *Ibid.*, p. 324.
57. *Ibid.*
58. *Ibid.*, p. 330.

3. *The Closed Novels*

1. *Satan in Goray* (New York: Noonday, 1955), p. 3.
2. Chmelnicki was a Cossack general who led an army "in insurrection against Polish landowners; enroute, they had fallen upon another target of their wrath, the Jewish townsfolk, the lords' stewards. It has been estimated that 100,000 Jews perished during the years from 1648 to 1658." (I quote from the translator's preface to *Satan in Goray*.)
3. *Satan in Goray*, p. 4.
4. Sabbatai Zevi was an Oriental Jew who, by means of an apostle, Nathan of Gaza, proclaimed the immediate salvation of the Jews. Many Jews accepted him as the Messiah. When confronted "by the Sultan with the choice between death and secular power," Sabbatai Zevi converted. He bebecame a Muslim and left the Jews "at the mercy of unprecedented inner dissension." (Again I quote from the translator's preface to *Satan in Goray*.)
5. *Satan in Goray*, p. 20.
6. *Ibid.*, p. 72.
7. *Ibid.*, p. 74.
8. *Ibid.*, p. 118.
9. *Ibid.*, p. 135.
10. *Ibid.*, p. 139.
11. *Ibid.*, p. 142.

12. *Ibid.*, p. 162.
13. *Ibid.*, p. 168.
14. *Ibid.*, p. 176.
15. *Ibid.*
16. *Ibid.*, p. 179.
17. *Ibid.*, p. 182.
18. *Ibid.*, p. 189.
19. *Ibid.*, p. 191.
20. *Ibid.*, p. 192.
21. *Ibid.*, p. 202.
22. *Ibid.*
23. *Ibid.*, p. 205.
24. *Ibid.*, p. 209.
25. *Ibid.*, p. 239.
26. *The Magician of Lublin* (New York: Noonday, 1960), p. 5.
27. *Ibid.*, p. 7.
28. *Ibid.*, p. 66.
29. *Ibid.*, p. 63.
30. *Ibid.*, p. 38.
31. *Ibid.*, p. 137.
32. *Ibid.*, p. 142.
33. *Ibid.*
34. *Ibid.*, p. 144.
35. *Ibid.*, p. 151.
36. *Ibid.*, p. 153.
37. *Ibid.*, p. 191.
38. *Ibid.*, p. 199.
39. *Ibid.*, p. 201.
40. *Ibid.*, p. 220.
41. *Ibid.*, p. 226.
42. *Ibid.*, p. 239.
43. *Ibid.*, p. 246.
44. *Ibid.*, p. 245.
45. *The Slave* (New York: Avon, 1962), p. 9.
46. *Ibid.*, p. 11. Both the Mishnah and the Gemara (commentary upon the Mishnah) comprise the Talmud, a literature of civil, religious, and ethical

lore completed in the 200's A.D. (for Mishnah) and 500's A.D. (for Gemara).

47. *Ibid.*, p. 12.
48. *Ibid.*, p. 38.
49. *Ibid.*
50. *Ibid.*, p. 39.
51. *Ibid.*, p. 55.
52. *Ibid.*
53. *Ibid.*
54. *Ibid.*, p. 99.
55. *Ibid.*
56. *Ibid.*, pp. 104-105.
57. *Ibid.*, p. 105.
58. *Ibid.*
59. *Ibid.*, p. 114.
60. *Ibid.*, p. 119.
61. *Ibid.*, p. 123. We are told that the Cossacks attack Poles and Jews. Jews continue to conduct business, supervising the tilling of leased fields, but they are viewed as survivors of Gentile struggles.
62. *Ibid.*, p. 143.
63. *Ibid.*, p. 163.
64. *Ibid.*, p. 190.
65. *Ibid.*, p. 193.
66. *Ibid.*, p. 200.
67. *Ibid.*
68. *Ibid.*, p. 227.
69. *Ibid.*
70. *Ibid.*
71. *Ibid.*, p. 228.
72. *Ibid.*
73. *Ibid.*, p. 234.
74. *Ibid.*, p. 233.
75. *Ibid.*, p. 248.
76. *Ibid.*, p. 250.
77. *Ibid.*, p. 252.
78. *Ibid.*
79. *Ibid.*, p. 253.

80. *Ibid.*, p. 254.
81. *Ibid.*

4.   *The Short Stories*

1. "Gimpel the Fool" in *Gimpel the Fool* (New York: Avon, 1965), p. 10.
2. *Ibid.*, p. 17.
3. *Ibid.*
4. *Ibid.*, p. 23.
5. *Ibid.*
6. *Ibid.*
7. *Ibid.*, p. 9.
8. *Ibid.*, p. 23.
9. "The Gentleman from Cracow" in *Gimpel the Fool*, p. 25.
10. *Ibid.*, p. 26.
11. *Ibid.*, p. 34.
12. *Ibid.*
13. *Ibid.*
14. *Ibid.*, p. 38.
15. *Ibid.*, pp. 40-41.
16. *Ibid.*, p. 41.
17. *Ibid.*, p. 42.
18. *Ibid.*, p. 79.
19. *Ibid.*
20. *Ibid.*, p. 81.
21. *Ibid.*, p. 83.
22. *Ibid.*, p. 87.
23. *Ibid.*, p. 88.
24. *Ibid.*, p. 96.
25. *Ibid.*, p. 103.
26. "The Spinoza of Market Street," *The Spinoza of Market Street* (New York: Avon, 1961), p. 8.
27. *Ibid.*, p. 9.
28. *Ibid.*, p. 12.
29. *Ibid.*, p. 14.

30. *Ibid.*
31. *Ibid.*, p. 7.
32. *Ibid.*, pp. 18-19.
33. *Ibid.*, p. 25.
34. *Ibid.*
35. *Ibid.*
36. *Ibid.*
37. "Shiddah and Kuziba," *The Spinoza of Market Street*, p. 83.
38. *Ibid.*
39. *Ibid.*
40. *Ibid.*, p. 84.
41. *Ibid.*, p. 86.
42. *Ibid.*
43. *Ibid.*, p. 87.
44. *Ibid.*, p. 88.
45. *Ibid.*
46. "The Black Wedding," *The Spinoza of Market Street*, p. 26.
47. *Ibid.*, pp. 29-30.
48. *Ibid.*, p. 30.
49. *Ibid.*, p. 31.
50. *Ibid.*, p. 33.
51. *Ibid.*, p. 35.
52. "The Man Who Came Back," *The Spinoza of Market Street*, p. 111.
53. *Ibid.*, p. 112.
54. *Ibid.*, p. 113.
55. *Ibid.*, p. 114.
56. *Ibid.*, p. 121.
57. *Ibid.*
58. *Ibid.*
59. "Blood," *Short Friday* (New York: Farrar, Straus and Giroux, 1964), p. 26.
60. *Ibid.*, p. 29.
61. *Ibid.*
62. *Ibid.*, p. 33.
63. *Ibid.*

64. *Ibid.*, p. 41.
65. *Ibid.*, p. 44.
66. *Ibid.*
67. *Ibid.*, p. 46.
68. *Ibid.*, p. 47.
69. "The Last Demon," *Short Friday*, p. 119.
70. *Ibid.*, p. 120.
71. *Ibid.*
72. *Ibid.*
73. *Ibid.*
74. *Ibid.*, p. 121.
75. *Ibid.*, p. 126.
76. *Ibid.*, p. 129.
77. *Ibid.*
78. "Short Friday," *Short Friday*, p. 229.
79. *Ibid.*, p. 230.
80. *Ibid.*, pp. 230-231.
81. *Ibid.*, p. 234.
82. *Ibid.*, p. 235.
83. *Ibid.*, p. 241.
84. *Ibid.*, p. 243.
85. "The Séance," *The Séance* (New York: Farrar, Straus, and Giroux, 1968), p. 3.
86. *Ibid.*, p. 9.
87. *Ibid.*, p. 11.
88. *Ibid.*
89. *Ibid.*
90. *Ibid.*, pp. 12-13.
91. *Ibid.*, p. 14.
92. *Ibid.*
93. *Ibid.*, p. 15.
94. *Ibid.*
95. *Ibid.*
96. *Ibid.*
97. "The Slaughterer," *The Séance*, pp. 19-20.
98. *Ibid.*, p. 20.
99. *Ibid.*, p. 21.
100. *Ibid.*

101. *Ibid.*, p. 23.
102. *Ibid.*, p. 24.
103. *Ibid.*, p. 26.
104. *Ibid.*
105. *Ibid.*, p. 30.
106 "Cockadoodledoo," *The Séance*, p. 85.
107. *Ibid.*, p. 86.
108. *Ibid.*, p. 87.
109. *Ibid.*, p. 89.
110. *Ibid.*
111. *Ibid.*, p. 92.
112. *Ibid.*
113. *Ibid.*, p. 93.
114. *Ibid.*, p. 94.
115. "Stories from Behind the Stove," *A Friend of Kafka* (New York: Farrar, Straus and Giroux, 1970), p. 66.
116. "The Cafeteria," *A Friend of Kafka*, p. 78.
117. *Ibid.*, p. 91.
118. *Ibid.*, p. 95.

Bibliography

Books by Isaac Bashevis Singer

The Family Moskat. Translated by A. H. Gross. New York: Knopf, 1950.

Satin in Goray. Translated by Jacob Sloan. New York: Noonday Press, 1955.

Gimpel the Fool and Other Stories. Translated by Saul Bellow, Isaac Rosenfeld, and others. New York: Noonday Press, 1957.

The Magician of Lublin. Translated by Elaine Gottlieb and Joseph Singer. New York: Noonday Press, 1960.

The Spinoza of Market Street. Translated by Martha Glicklich and others. New York: Farrar, Straus and Cudahy, 1961.

The Slave. Translated by the author and Cecil Hemley. New York: Farrar, Straus and Cudahy, 1962.

Short Friday and Other Stories. Translated by Joseph Singer, Roger Klein, and others. New York: Farrar, Straus, and Giroux, 1964.

In My Father's Court. Translated by Channah Kleinerman-Goldstein and others. New York: Farrar, Straus and Giroux, 1966.

The Manor. Translated by Joseph Singer and Elaine Gottlieb. New York: Farrar, Straus, and Giroux, 1967.

The Séance and Other Stories. Translated by Roger
    Klein, Cecil Hemley, and others. New York: Farrar,
    Straus and Giroux, 1968.
The Estate. Translated by Joseph Singer, Elaine Gottlieb,
    and Elizabeth Shub. New York: Farrar, Straus and
    Giroux, 1969.
A Friend of Kafka and Other Stories. Translated by the
    author, Elizabeth Shub, and others. New York: Far-
    rar, Straus and Giroux, 1970.

Uncollected Essays and Reviews
by Isaac Bashevis Singer

"The Everlasting Joke," *Commentary* (May 1961), 458-
    460.
"The Extreme Jews," *Harper's* (April 1967), 55-62.
"Introduction" to *The Adventures of One Yitzchok* by
    Yitzchok Perlov. New York: Award Books, 1967.
    7-12.
"Introduction" to *Hunger* by Knut Hamsun. New York:
    Noonday Press, 1968. v-xii.
"Introduction" to *Yoshe Kalb* by I. J. Singer. New York:
    Harper and Row, 1965. pp. v-x.
"Realism and Truth," *Reconstructionist* (June 15, 1962),
    5-9.
"Rootless Mysticism," *Commentary* (January 1965), 77-
    78.
"What It Takes to Be a Jewish Writer," *National Jewish
    Monthly* (November 1963), 54-56.

Books about Isaac Bashevis Singer

Allentuck, Marcia, ed. *The Achievement of Isaac Bashevis
    Singer*. Carbondale: Southern Illinois University
    Press, 1970.
Buchen, Irving H. *Isaac Bashevis Singer and the Eternal*

Past. New York: New York University Press, 1968.

Malin, Irving, ed. *Critical Views of Isaac Bashevis Singer.* New York: New York University Press, 1969.

Siegel, Ben. *Isaac Bashevis Singer.* Minneapolis: University of Minnesota Press, 1969.

Essays about Isaac Bashevis Singer

Elman, Richard M. "The Spinoza of Canal Street," *Holiday* (August 1965), 83-87.

Frank, M. Z. "The Demon and the Earlock," *Conservative Judaism* (Fall 1965), 1-9.

Glatstein, Jacob. "The Fame of Bashevis Singer," *Congress Bi-Weekly* (December 27, 1965), 17-19.

Hemley, Cecil. "Isaac Bashevis Singer" in *Dimensions of Midnight: Poetry and Prose*, ed. Elaine Gottlieb. Athens: Ohio University Press, 1966. pp. 217-33.

Hindus, Milton. "Isaac Bashevis Singer" in *Jewish Heritage Reader*, ed. Morris Adler. New York: Taplinger, 1965. pp. 242-252.

Hughes, Ted. "The Genius of Isaac Bashevis Singer," *New York Review of Books* (April 22, 1965), 8-10.

Hyman, Stanley Edgar. "Isaac Singer's Marvels," *New Leader* (December 21, 1964), 17-18.

Kazin, Alfred. "The Saint as Schlemiel" in *Contemporaries*. Boston: Little, Brown, 1962. pp. 283-91.

Madison, Charles A. "I. Bashevis Singer: Novelist of Hasidic Gothicism," in *Yiddish Literature, Its Scope and Major Writers*. New York: Frederick Ungar Publishing Co., 1968. pp. 479-499.

Pinsker, Sanford. "The Isolated Schlemiels of Isaac Bashevis Singer" in *The Schlemiel as Metaphor*. Carbondale: Southern Illinois University Press, 1971. pp. 55-87.

Pondrom, Cyrena N. "Isaac Bashevis Singer: An Interview," *Contemporary Literature* (Winter, Summer, 1969), 1-38, 32-51.

Siegel, Ben. "Sacred and Profane: Isaac Bashevis Singer's Embattled Spirits," *Critique* (Spring 1963), 24-47.

Sloan, Jacob. "I. B. Singer and his Yiddish Critics," *Congress Bi-Weekly* (March 7, 1966), 4-5.

For a more complete bibliography the reader should consult Jackson R. Bryer and Paul E. Rockwell, "Isaac Bashevis Singer in English: A Bibliography" in the collection edited by Irving Malin.

Index